I0755835

Cocktails & Conversation

Written By:
Izzy The Mixologist

Table of Contents

Introduction

Writing a book wasn't always apart of the plan. During that time, I lost the ambition of making a better life for myself. Some days I was happy but most days I felt like I was a magnet to everything negative. At the age of 25, I was done with what life was offering me. Not only did I need change I desperately wanted change so I did something about it. I booked a one-way ticket to Atlanta and I knew this would be the start of my faith journey. I was leaving my home town not knowing what life had in store for me, but rest assure I was going to find out. 2 months of me being in Atlanta I found a job that I had no idea would change my life forever. I worked as a bartender prior but I didn't have any knowledge about what a craft cocktail consisted of. I gained so much knowledge about the art and I was immediately intrigued. I learned very quickly and I was strikingly good at it. As I continued to work on my craft, I began to come up with ideas to create a business and a brand.

Every cocktail in this book is created by yours truly to celebrate the passage of time. Every season brings new reflections. In Summer we enjoy classic cocktails while discussing the ins and outs of romantic relationship. In Autumn I'll cover some bold cocktails to help you embrace change. In Spring I'll show you some lightweight cocktails to refresh you on your journey of decluttering. The final chapter on Winter brings a feeling of warmness and coziness, the perfect time to indulge in sweet delights.

Bar Tools

Shaker
Mixing glass
Jigger
Julep Strainer
Fine mesh strainer
Hawthornette strainer
Muddler
Bar spoon
Knife
Peeler
Ball digger
Poor spouts
Measuring cup
Funnel
Juicer
Dehydrator
Blender
Torch
Cedar planks

Chapter 1
Who tf is Izzy the Mixologist

Nine years ago, I worked at a small boutique hotel as a front desk agent. We had a restaurant inside the hotel with a full-service bar. One of the bartenders quit and I was given the opportunity to take their place. I was young and scared to say the least, but I went with it. I learned the basics and earned the title of bartender. I didn't know much about cocktails but I was determined to learn as much as I could in a small amount of time. I saw how much the guests loved the other bartender so I strived to get that same respect. As time went on, I got better and better. I started to get compliments like "this is the best margarita I've ever had". Compliments like this always wowed me because I knew how important it was for guests to enjoy their bartender, as well as their favorite cocktail.

One of my favorite cocktails to make back then was a Miami vice. It's two cocktails in one and was perfect for the hot summer days. The Miami Vice was one of our best sellers, especially for the ladies. As a two-tone creation, it made for a beautiful cocktail. It made us feel like being on a private island. This was the cocktail that gave me the confidence to keep going in this industry.

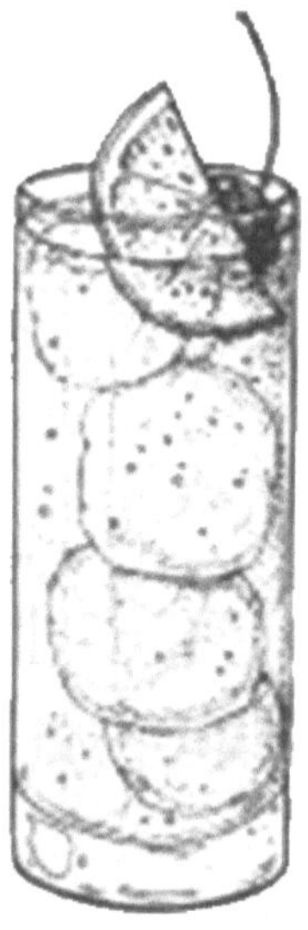

Miami Vice

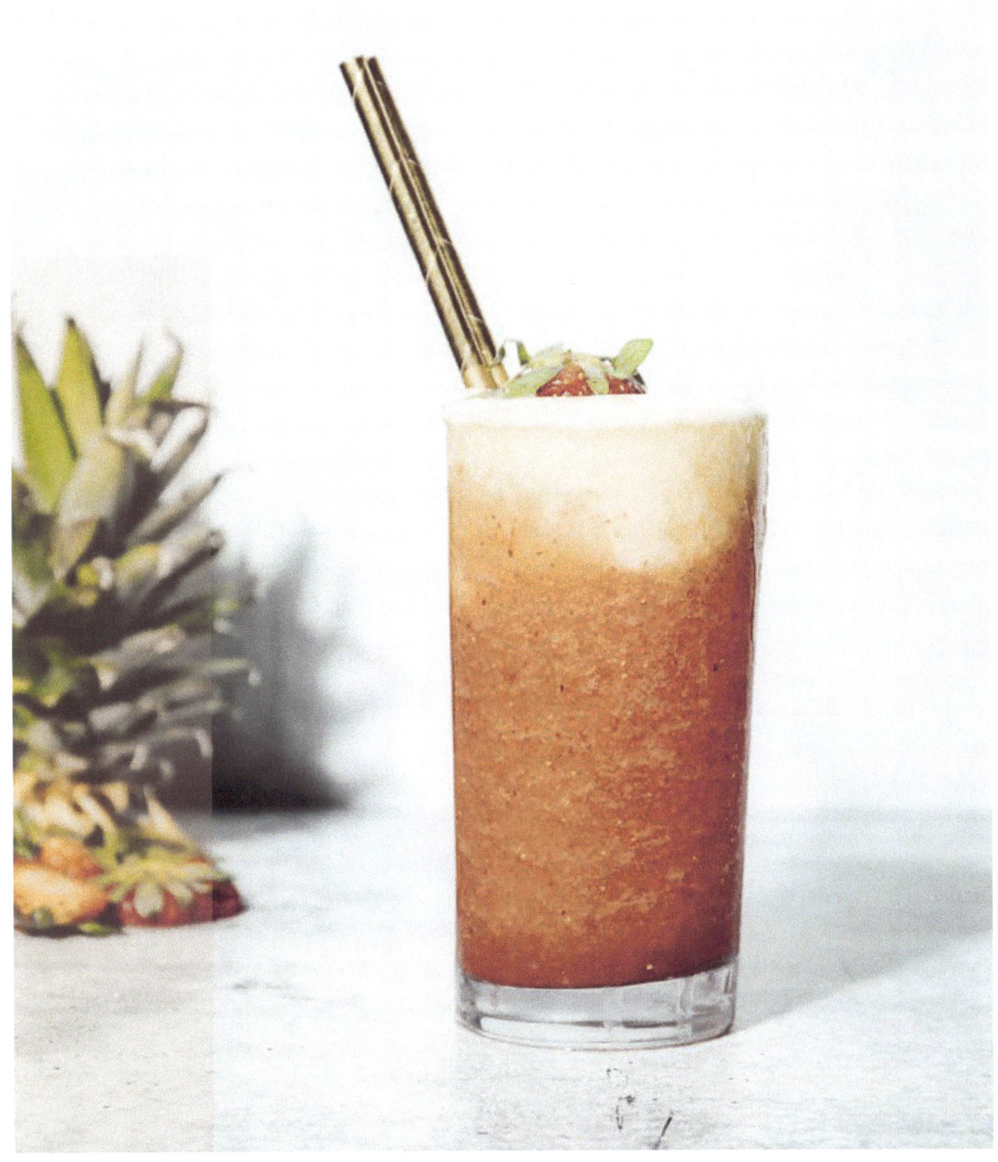

Ingredients:	Instructions:
• 1oz rum • ½ cup fresh strawberries chopped • 1oz fresh lime juice • 2oz simple syrup • 1oz coconut rum • 2oz cream of coconut • ½ fresh pineapple chopped • Garnish with strawberry	• Add both cocktail ingredients in separate blenders or do 1 by 1 • Add crushed ice • Blend until thick and smooth • Start by pouring 1 cocktail in glass half way • Pour second slowly to top it off • Add garnish and straw

After 5 years of working at the hotel I decided it was time to move on. I started working at a resort as a front desk agent. I worked there for a year then realized I was completely unhappy. I didn't know what I wanted for myself but I knew I needed change. One day, without telling anyone I booked a one-way ticket to Atlanta. Looking back, that was the best decision I could have ever made for myself. I left many saddened and worried but I had to do what was best for me regardless of their opinions or approval.

During this period, I learned about many classic cocktails. My favorite to drink was the lemon drop. It was a step up from the frozen cocktails and it made me feel mature and classy. When it's made right it can be the perfect martini. It's the perfect balance of sweet and tart, and with a sugared rim you can't go wrong. I was young and going through an existential crisis and the Lemon Drop played a big part of me figuring out my life.

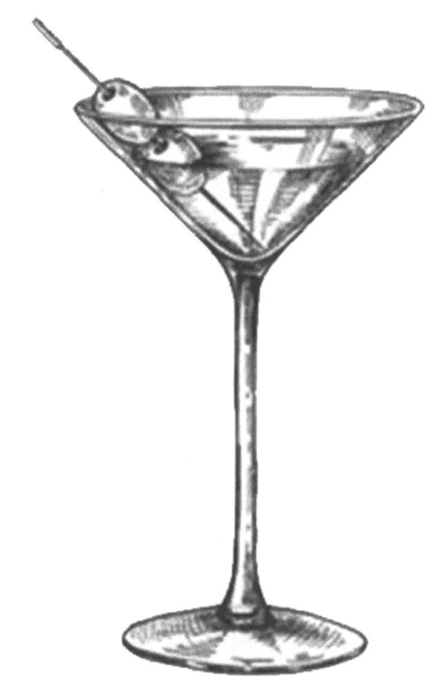

Lemon Drop Martini

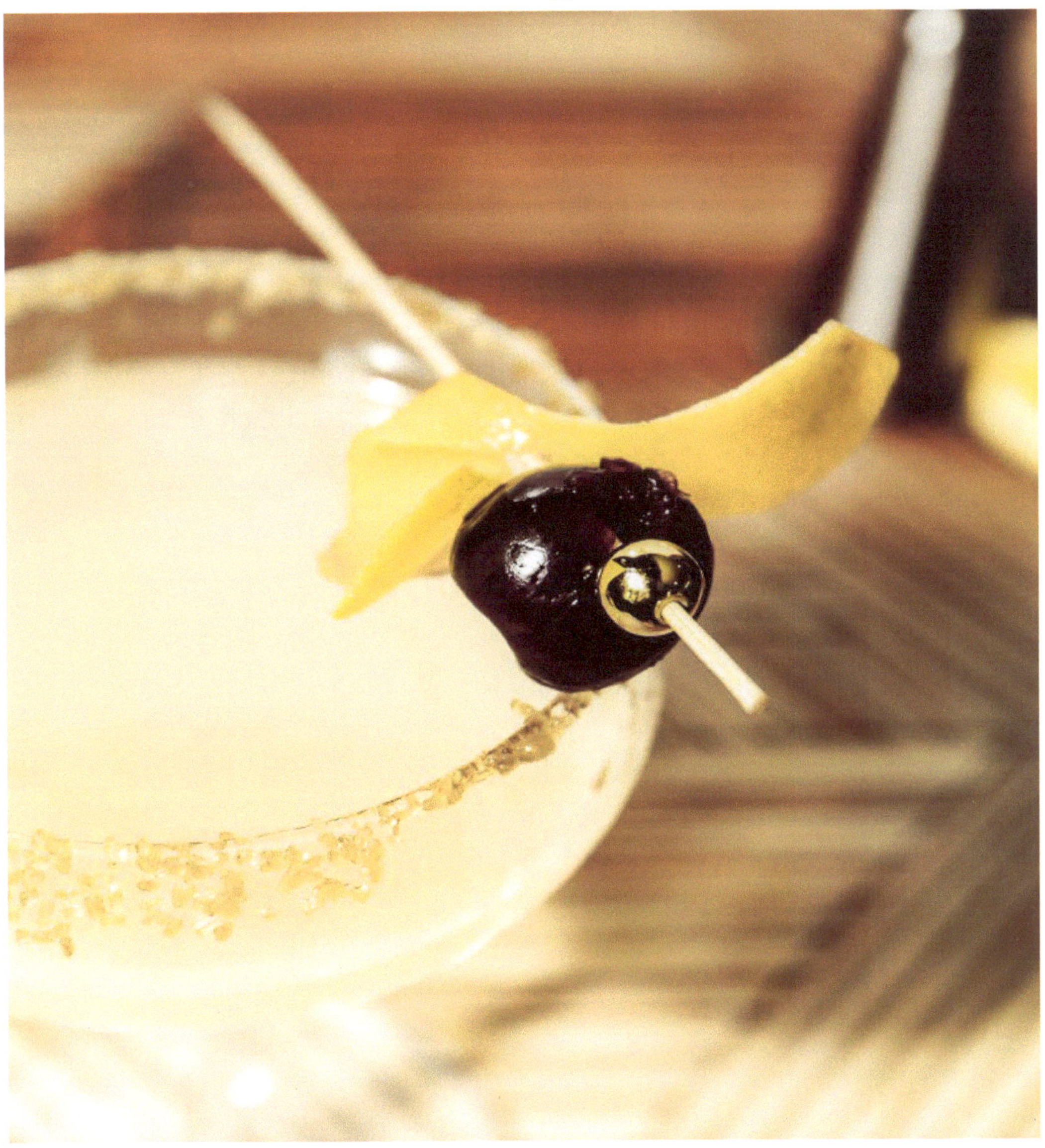

Ingredients:	Instructions:
• 2 oz vodka • 1oz simple syrup • 1oz fresh lemon juice • 2 dash orange bitters	• Rim glass with sugar • Add ice to coupe glass to chill • Add all ingredients to shaker • Add ice and shake • Dump ice out of glass • Strain cocktail into glass • Garnish with lemon twist and cherry

Simple Syrup: 1:1 Sugar and Water

So here I am! I made it to Atlanta. I'm in a big city with endless opportunities. I'm starting over with a few boxes of clothes and a jalopy of a car. I couldn't believe I'd left California. I was away from my family but that became my motivation. I started looking for work immediately, surprisingly it didn't take long. I came across a hotel that wasn't quite open yet and was looking for people immediately. It was just my luck that they called me back the next day. I started out as a waitress but I fought hard to be behind the bar full time. At this point it wasn't because of the title, it was solely for the money.

Once I got behind the bar, I soon realized that I was being introduced to a whole new world of cocktails. I thought I knew everything there was to know about bartending, but I only knew the basics. Saying yes to this first opportunity was all intentional for laying my foundation in the mixology world. My colleague Cody took me under his wing and taught me everything I needed to know about craft cocktails. I learned a lot from the importance of a jigger to developing a love for the Aperol spritz. The Aperol spritz is refreshing and bubbly, making for the perfect cocktail all year long.

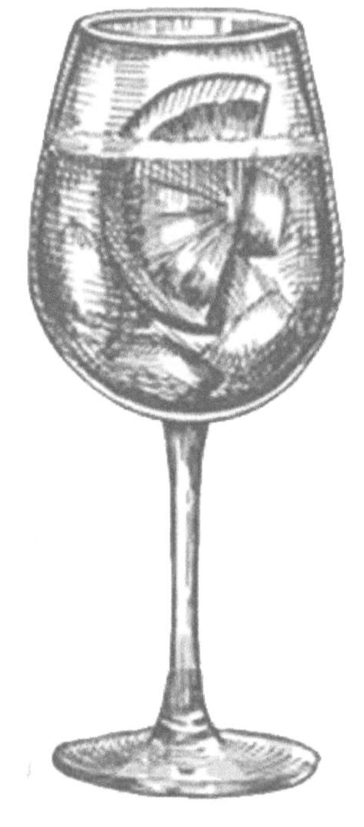

Aperol Spritz

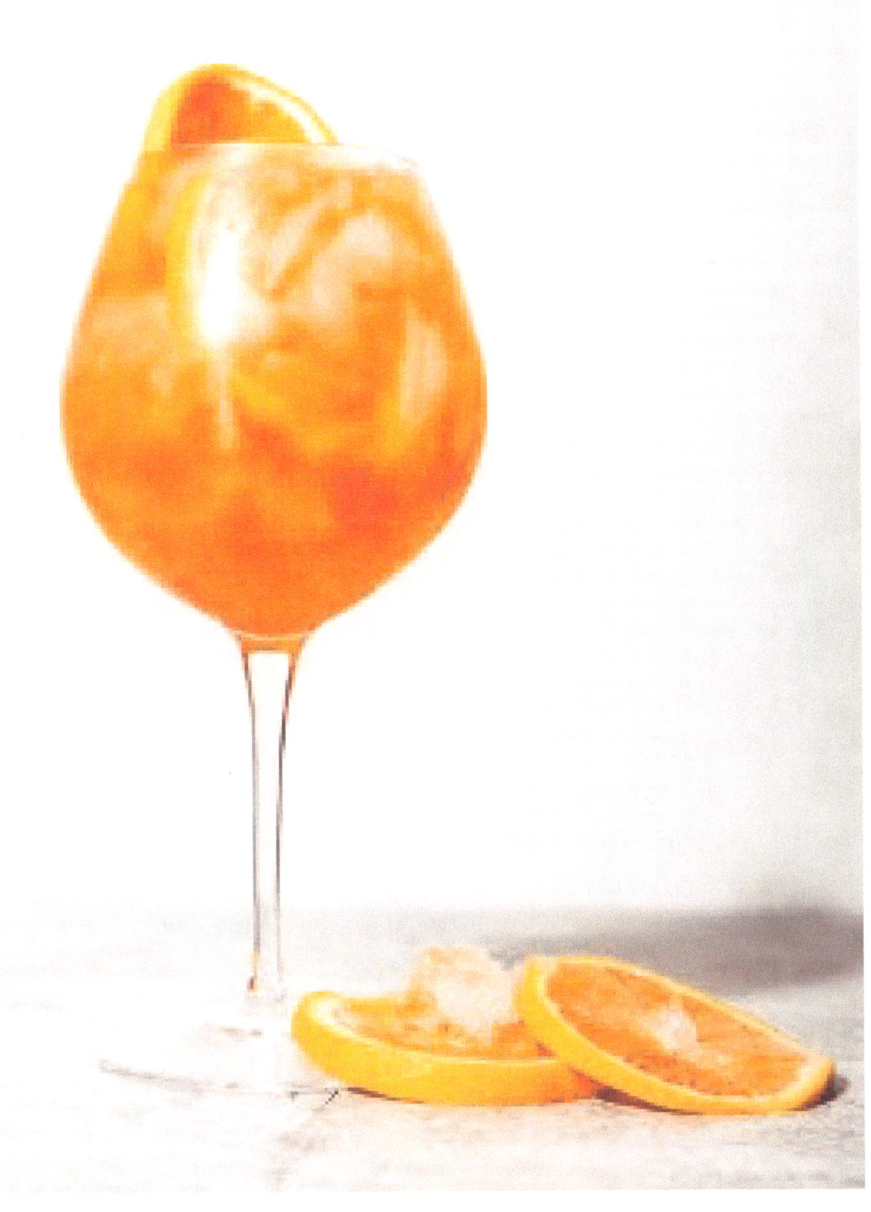

Ingredients:	Instructions:
• 2 parts Aperol • 3 parts prosecco • 2 parts club soda	• Fill wine glass with crushed ice • Add all ingredients directly into glass • Top with a little more ice • Add sliced oranges to cocktail

After 2 years in, it was no longer just about the money, I'd found my passion. From learning, to the process of creation it was all liberating to me. Every time I went to work, I wanted to create a new cocktail. I wanted the guests to love my creations so much that I started an at home bar to practice. I invested the small amount of money I had and bought as many spirits as I could to experiment with. Little by little I would buy other tools that would take my cocktails to the next level. Of course, I couldn't afford a real bar but the kitchen counter tops held my bottles nicely. My kitchen looked like World War II but I couldn't make excuses if I wanted to grow in this industry. At the time I had two roommates that would do the honor of trying all my cocktails and give me the real. Most were a go but some weren't and that was the beauty of trial and error.

I had become so invested in my craft that I had to figure out a way to turn my passion into a long-term business and brand. I came up with the idea of catering private events, giving people the experience they were missing. I still strive to enact this dream, I can thank my all-time favorite cocktail for the inspiration. The old fashioned is simple but delicious. It's a sipping cocktail which makes for a chill night. This was my go to when I needed to wind down and tap into my creative space. The classic cocktail can be experimented with in so many ways but still be simple. It helped me take the edge off when creating became stressful. It reminded me that you don't have to do much to create an amazing cocktail.

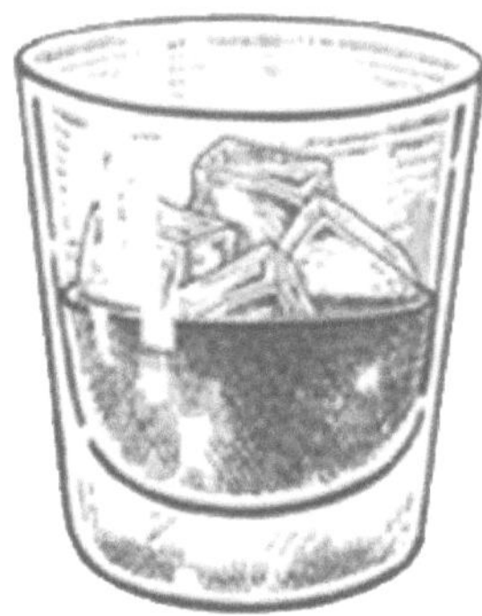

The Smokey Old Fashioned

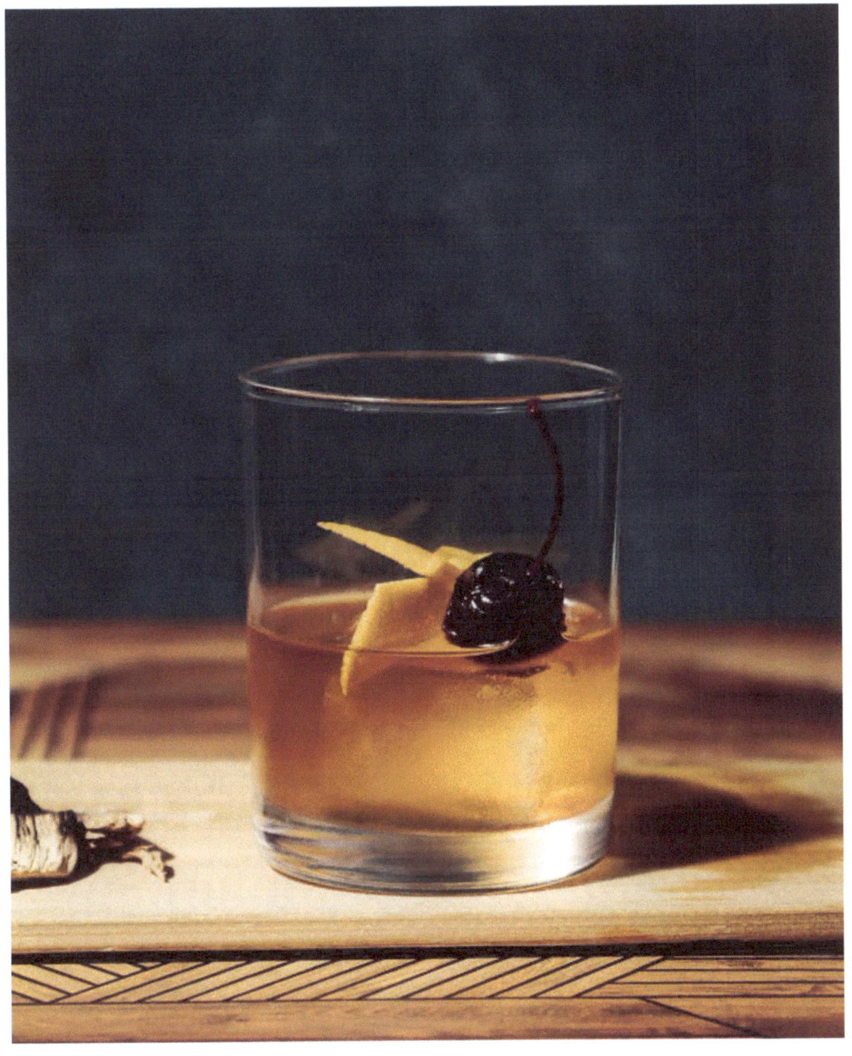

Ingredients:	Instructions:
• 2oz Bourbon • ½ oz honey syrup • 2 dash orange bitters • 2 dash angostura bitters	• Smoke wood chips with torch and place glass on top • Add all ingredients to mixing glass • Fill with ice • Stir with bar spoon until ice dilutes • Strain into rocks glass • Add large rock • Garnish with orange peel and bourbon cherry
• Honey Syrup: 1:1 honey and hot water	

It's 2021 and I find myself having the same passion years later. I have goals that I've reached and goals that I have yet to accomplish but I haven't given up. The truth is, it hasn't been an easy journey. I've learned so much about myself during the process good and bad. Writing this book has been on the to do list for some time now. It was a vision I had in the beginning but could never get right. I didn't know what I wanted to say or even where to start for that matter. One day while
sitting around my table with friends and family enjoying conversation over drinks, a new hot topic had entered the convo when someone said "wait we all need another cocktail for this topic". At that very moment that's when I knew what I wanted to say and how I wanted to say it. I couldn't believe that I didn't have this idea sooner because cocktails and conversation are a part of our everyday lives. I now had to trust God's timing and what he wanted to do in my life and envision for my book.

At this point in the game, I've tried so many amazing classic craft cocktails and created so many of my own that I have lots of favorites. I enjoy cocktails that are strong, bitter and a tad bit sweet. The first cocktail that comes to my mind when I think of this flavor profile is the boulevardier. It describes what I love to the tee. It has been at the top of the list of my favorites for a while now.

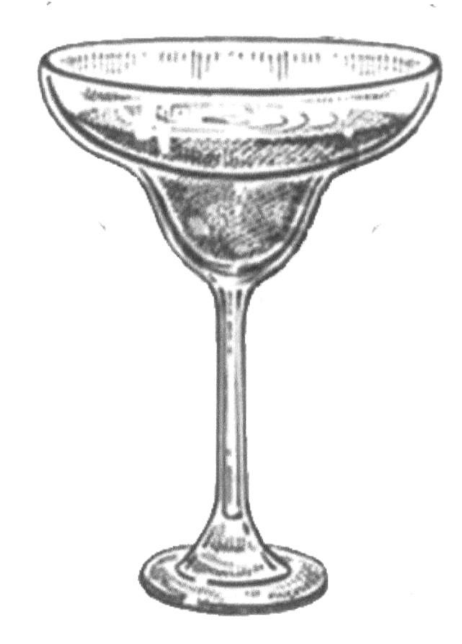

Boulevardier

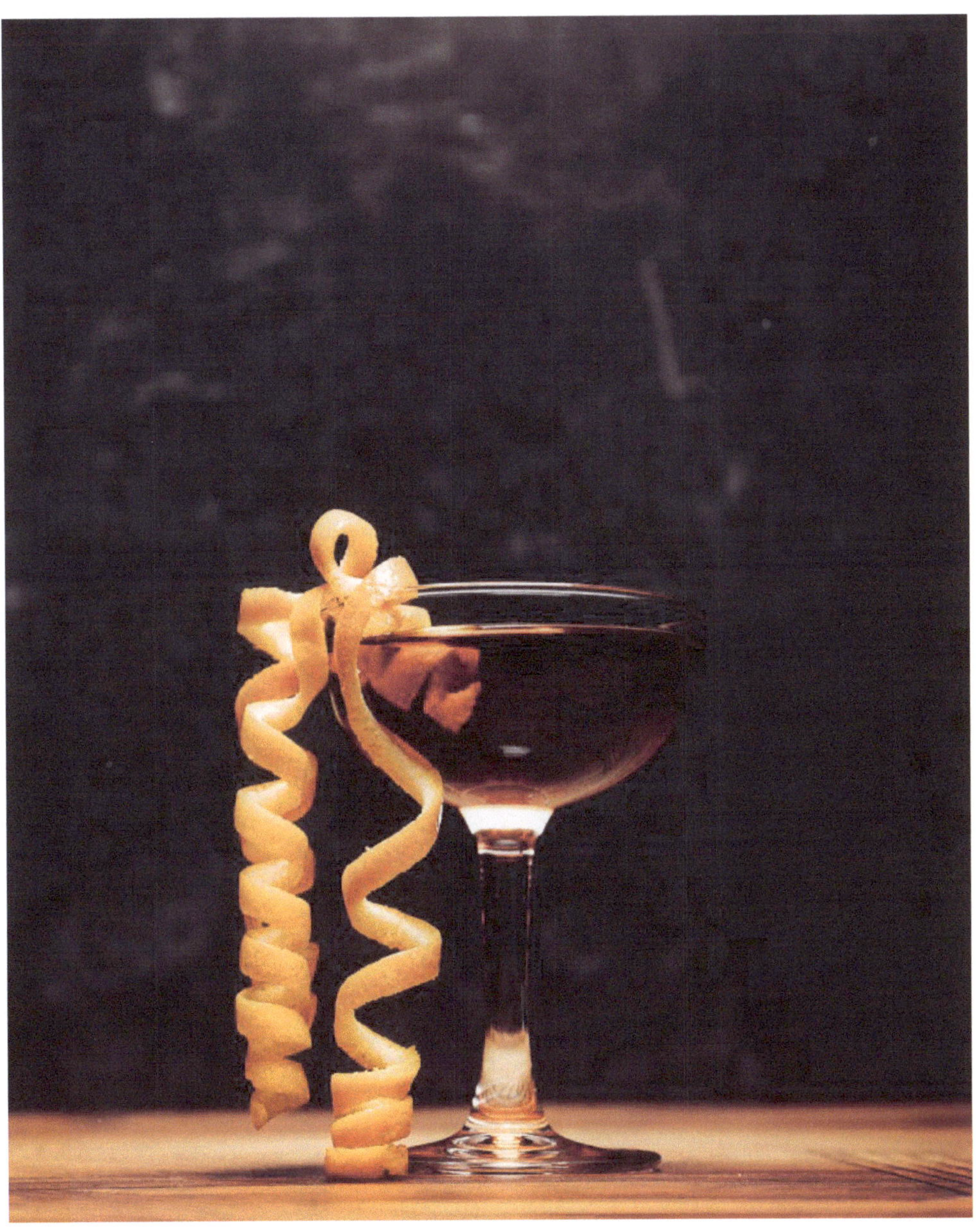

Ingredients:	Instructions:
• 1oz bourbon • 1oz Campari • 1oz sweet vermouth	• Add all ingredients to mixing glass • Stir until ice dilutes • Strain into coupe glass • Garnish with orange peel

Chapter 2
Baby you Summertime Fine

The heat brings out characteristics in people that make you want to be single. I can admit I'm one of the ones who thinks less clothes is better. It's cute and it's the season for it. I never thought anything was wrong with wearing skimpy clothing as long as you were confident and comfortable in your own skin.

The "Skinny Dip" is the perfect cocktail to get your hot girl, hot boy summer started. If you're ready to show off some skin but keep your figure popping all summer long you will love this sugarless cocktail.

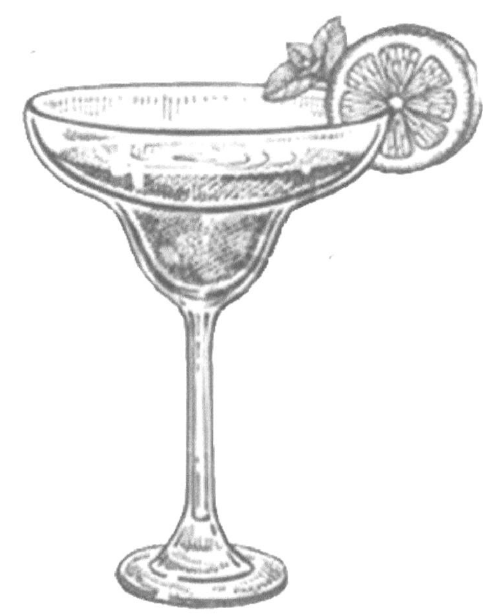

Skinny Dip

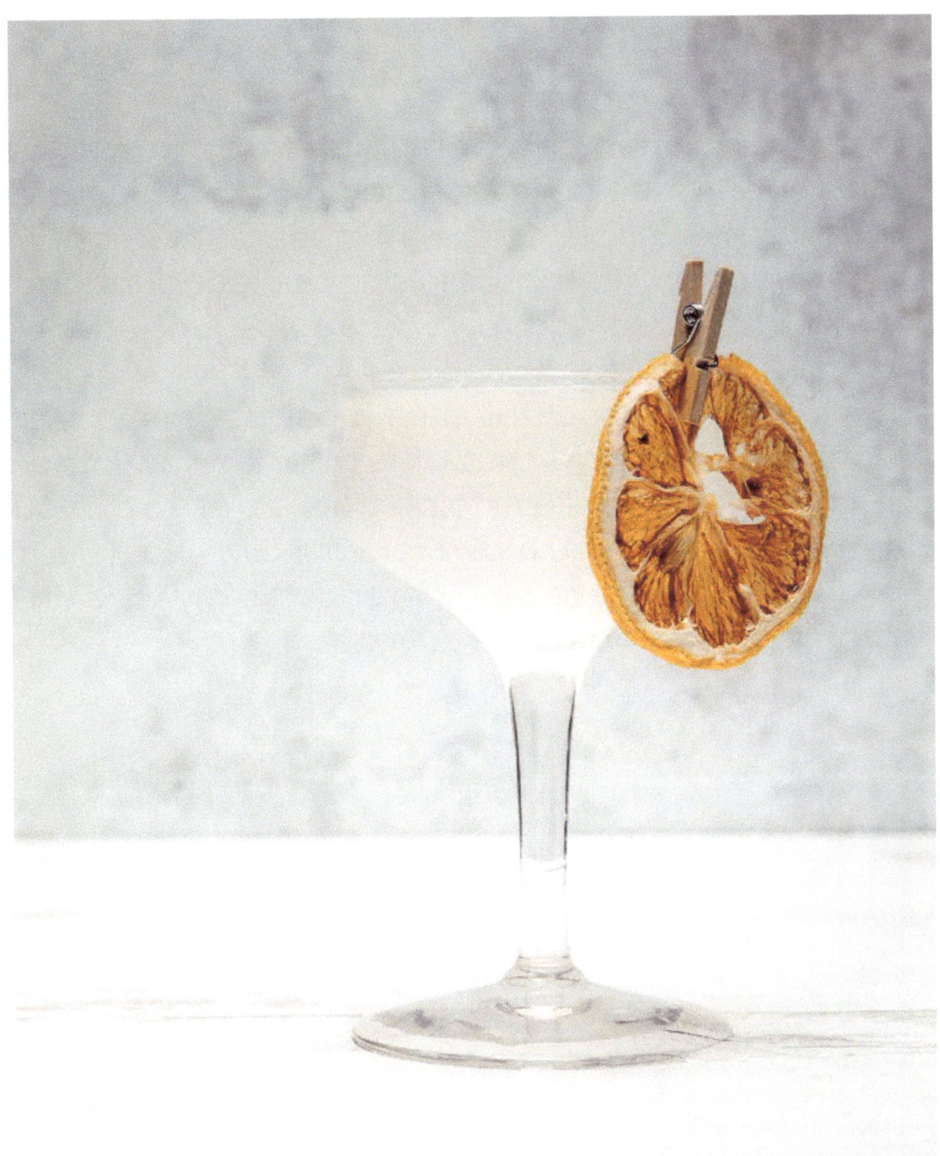

Ingredients:	Instructions:
• 1.5oz Peach Orange Blossom Ketel One • 2oz Coconut water • .5oz Lemon Juice	• Add ice to coupe glasses and let it chill • Add all ingredients to shaker • Shake until ice dilutes • Dump ice out of coupe glass • Strain the cocktail into the chilled glass • Garnish with dehydrated lemon wheel

Let's be honest though, men and women are not the same. Everyone's beliefs are different. We all believe in something which means we all have our own opinions. People on the internet don't know who you are so prepare to be judged. Different religions don't understand your beliefs and don't have to, so again prepare to be judged.

The margarita is a classic cocktail that most people love. If it's made improperly it can be a very big turn off similar to how others' opinions may not add up to what we believe to be true. It's ok to do you as long as you're ok with the decisions you make for your own life. This margarita is the perfect example of "dare to be different". It's my take on the classic margarita, I promise it'll be your new favorite.

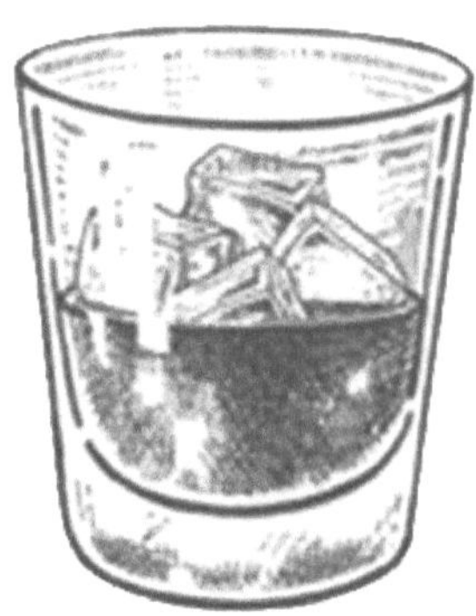

The Hot Mama Margarita

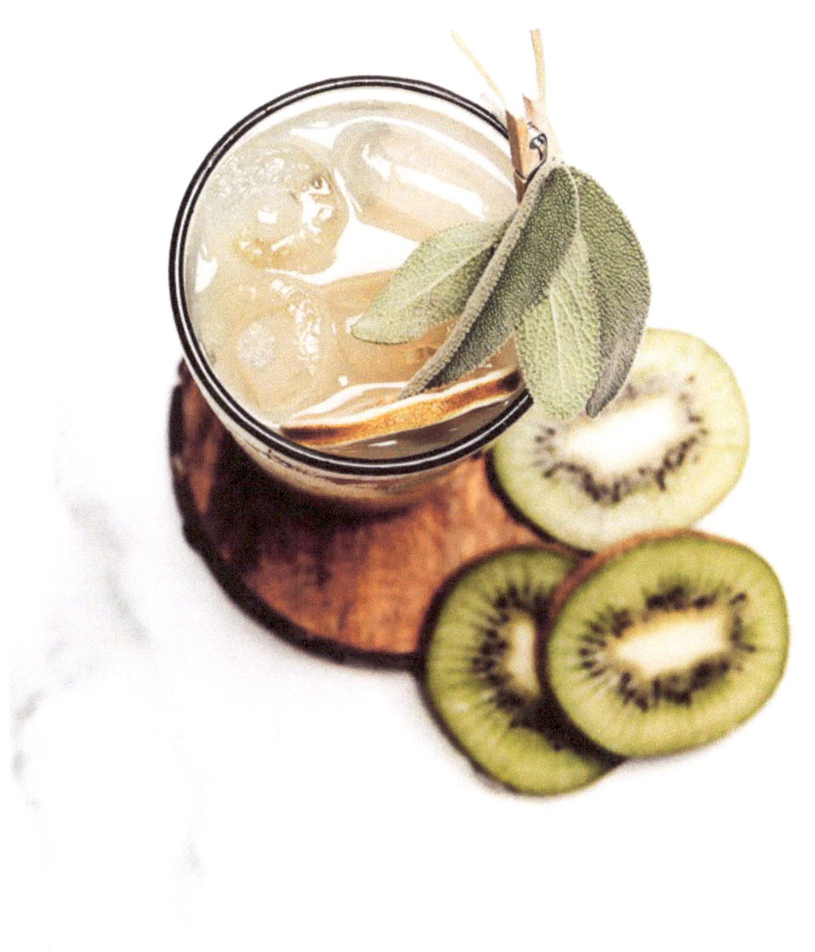

Ingredients:	Instructions:
• 2oz Mezcal • 1oz Grand Marnier • 1oz Kiwi Sage Syrup • .5oz Fresh Lime	• Add all ingredients into shaker • Fill with ice • Shake vigorously until ice dilutes • Strain into glass over fresh ice • Garnish with fresh sage and kiwi slices

Kiwi Sage Simple Syrup: 1 cup freshly squeezed kiwi juice, 1 cup fresh sage, ½ cup sugar

Men are not blind to beautiful women. Hell, if your ass is hanging out, they're still going to look whether you're cute or not. As women we see how fine we look in short shorts and crop tops and it's just that, but men's minds go straight to sex. Men have insecurities that aren't always displayed because they're taught to hold a lot in. Do you know how mad men get when their woman is out here for everyone to look at? It makes them question your value and causes them to be petty, and then they have to go feed their ego in another woman's pants. Once the petty starts this is when women feel the heat. Women are strong enough to be in a relationship and get attention from other men and remain faithful. This is why we don't understand why it matters what we wear. Truth is men can't deal with the stress they cause us.

Now this cocktail is perfect for this conversation. Gin is one of those spirits that is enjoyed by both men and women. Its floral and sweet notes bring refreshing flavors to any cocktail making it very popular in the summertime. Pairing Gin with fresh ingredients really brings out the botanicals in gin. Hence why we have quite a lot going on in this cocktail, much like the issues we deal with when it comes to the insecurities within relationships.

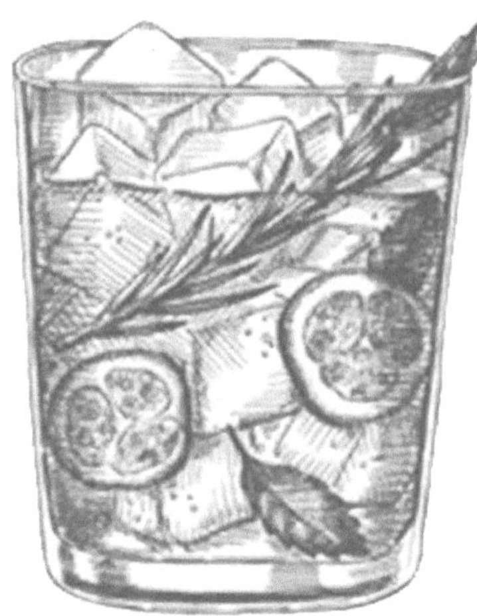

Hotel, Motel, Holiday Inn

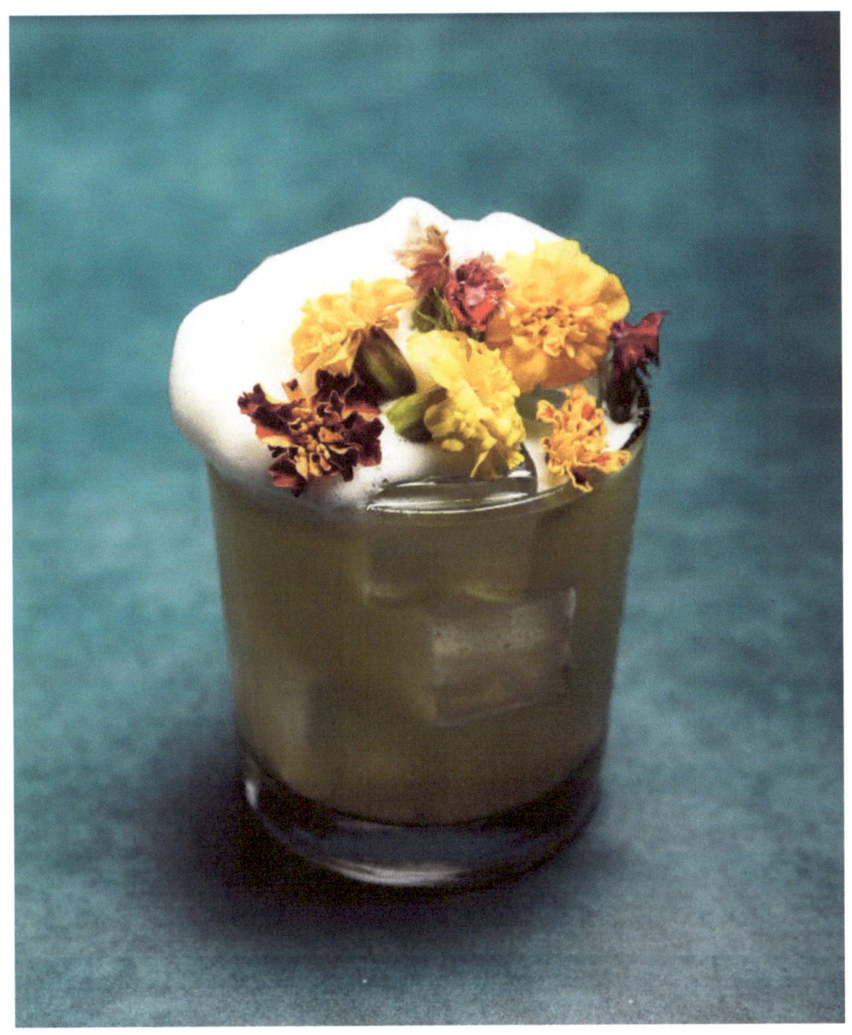

Ingredients:	Instructions:
• 2oz Gin • 1oz St Germain • .25oz Midori • 1oz fresh lemon juice • ½ Muddled Kiwi • Egg whites •	• Add fresh lemon and kiwi to shaker and muddle • Add all other ingredients including egg whites • Shake vigorously without ice for 20 seconds • Add a small amount of ice and shake hard for another 20 seconds • Double strain into rocks glass over fresh ice • Garnish with edible flowers

Let's not get it twisted now. There are men out there who are secure in themselves and their woman and vice versa. Loving on yourself and truly loving your partner can require a lot of labor. I'm convinced that God is definitely involved in these types of relationships because you don't see healthy relationships often. People don't want to put the work in to have a relationship with God because they're distracted by toxicity. Being on the same page with someone doesn't just come from the strength of two beings. God gives them the strength to fight for understanding, wisdom, courage, trust and everything else desired in a healthy relationship.

New cocktails remind me of a healthy relationship. If it doesn't sound good chances are you won't try it, but just imagine what could have come out of it if you did try it. This shrub cocktail is a representation of taking your relationship to the next level and continuing to do the work for a healthier outcome in your relationships.

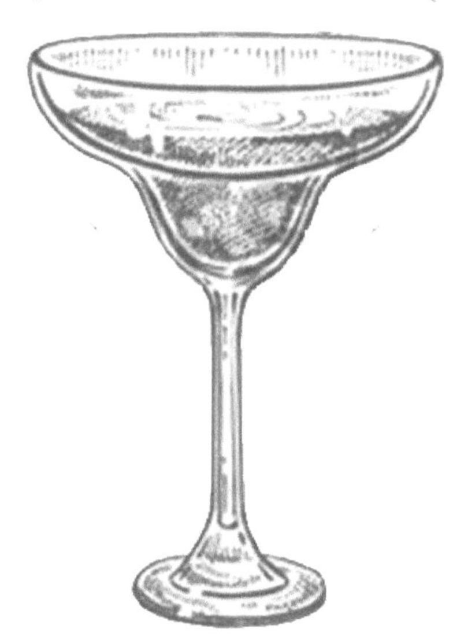

Flamingo Beach

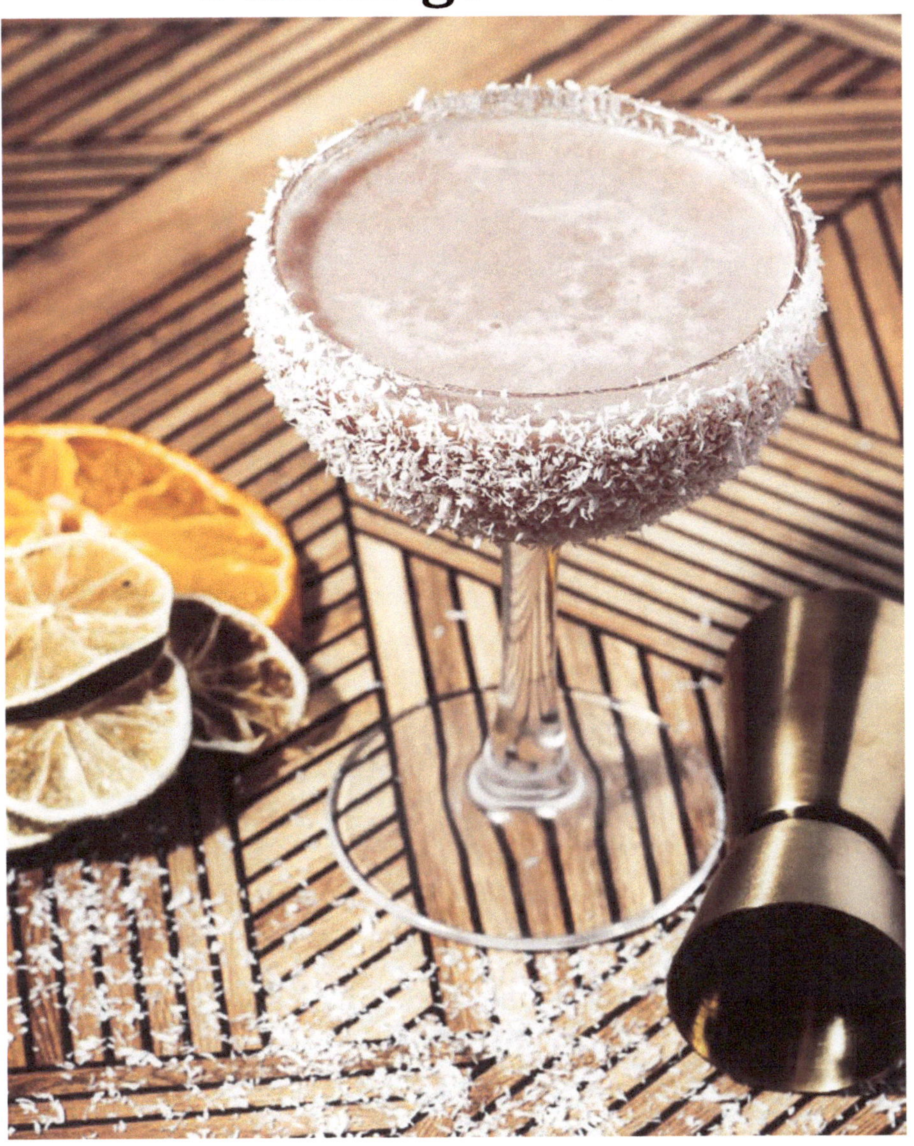

Ingredients:	Instructions:
• 1oz coconut rum • 1oz white rum • 1oz raspberry shrub • 1 bar spoon cream of coconut	• Coat entire glass with honey and sprinkle coconut flakes all over • Add ice to coupe glass to chill • Add all ingredients to shaker and shake vigorously • Dump ice and double strain into coupe glass • Sprinkle coconut flakes on top

Rasberry shrub: 1 cup of fresh raspberries, ½ cup apple cider vinegar, ½ cup sugar
Let it sit for 24 hours

I know It seems like I'm beating up on men but believe me, I'm not blind to what women are capable of. Men aren't the only ones who cheat. Women cheat too and not all of us have genuine intentions. I've never been the type to want anything other than love and commitment from a man. Some women won't settle for a man who's not coming out of pocket and most of these women are winning. I don't know everyone's story but to a certain degree I understand the woman who looks past the love and commitment. Hurt is a mf and it makes you want to be the savage woman. Me on the other hand, I'm team love 100%. Sometimes I wish I had that savage mindset in me because then hurt from a man would be non-existent. The reality is we all settle for things we don't really want because we don't want to be patient.

I'm a right now type of person so patience isn't my strongest attribute, especially in relationships. My problem is that I think each man is going to be better than the previous one. I give my all every single time and end up with the same results in the end. It doesn't matter if you're crazy or cool. If a man doesn't want to be there he won't. I can count a good two times where hurt from a man caused me to be the savage woman. Being a savage isn't in me, I was just pushed to the limit. I did what I thought would feel good in that moment, and I played myself in the end. There's no balance between the red flags and what I deserve. If you're a person like me who needs to work on patience and balance in those situations, this will be your go to cocktail. The cocktail is sweet and sour, topped with a juicy rose. Anything too sweet or sour is never enjoyable so you have to add something that will balance it right? If figuring out your worth is the last option, pack your bags and hit the road. Know that just like this cocktail you are the perfect balance whether they like you or not. Remember baby, you're summer time fine.

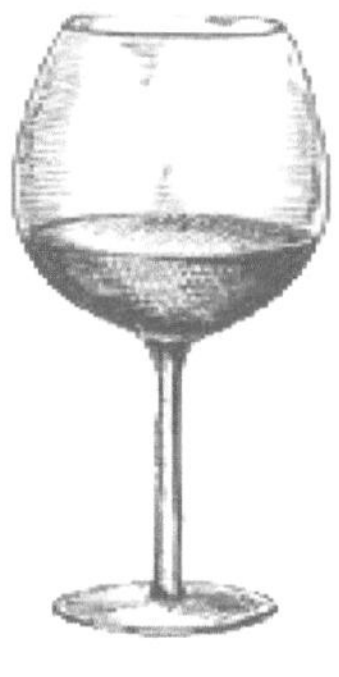

A Balanced Summer

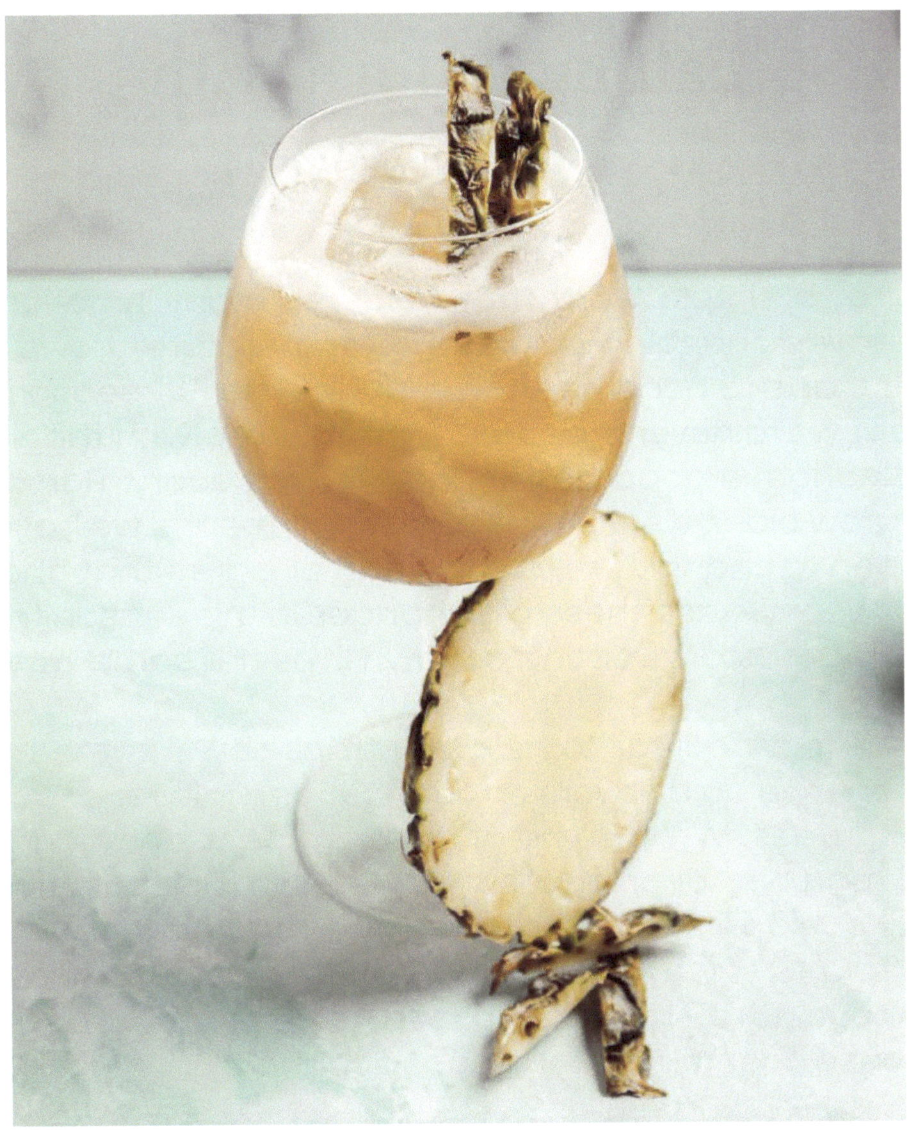

Ingredients:	Instructions:
• 2oz Tequila Blanco • 2oz Thai Basil Plum Shrub • 1oz Fresh Pineapple juice • 2oz Rose	• Add all ingredients to the Shaker • Fill with ice and shake vigorously • Pour cocktail along with dirty ice into wine glass • Garnish with pineapple
Thai Basil Plum Shrub: Piedmont Provisions	

Chapter 3
Falling in love with Autumn

Change...what a simple word that holds so many emotions. You see trees and leaves changing colors, the temperature grows colder and the daylight starts to become shorter during the Fall season. These are changes that we're never prepared for but we go with the flow anyways. Change is good but change is also scary. Personally, I find that as we grow older, we gain wisdom which means we have no choice but to be open to change. I'm sure we can all agree that change is taboo. Every year we see these big changes in this season that we can't control so why not start treating our own lives the same way.

This is the perfect cocktail to help you transition into the new season. You will experience bold flavors throughout and a layer of colors just like the changing trees. While some of us might be used to our margaritas and classic martinis, fall cocktails are diverse in their bold flavor profiles. In these fall cocktails you'll see spirits like rum, cognac and bourbon. Don't be afraid to shy away from what you're used to and fall more in love with fall cocktails. Not to mention fall is my favorite season so I hope you enjoy these cocktails as much as I do.

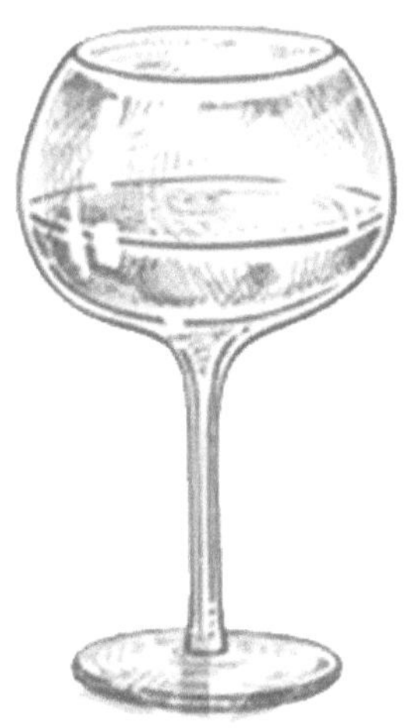

Autumn Nights

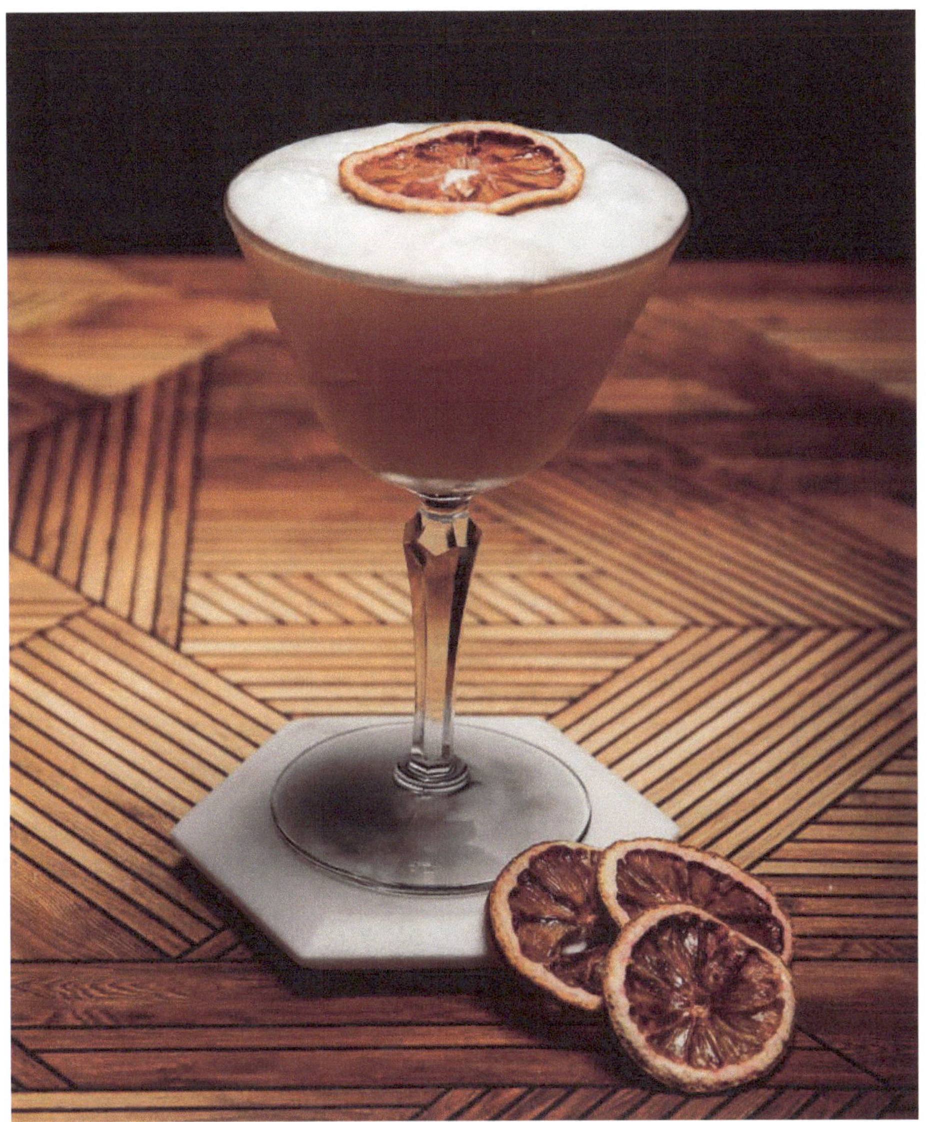

Ingredients:	Instructions:
• 1.5oz Bacardi Gold • 1oz Cointreau Noir • 1oz Blood Orange Simple Syr-up • 1oz Lemon Juice • 1oz Pineapple • Egg whites	• Add all ingredients to shaker with egg whites • Dry shaker hard without ice for 20 seconds • Fill shaker with ice and shake hard for another 20 seconds • Strain into coupe glass • Garnish with dehydrated blood orange

Blood Orange Simple Syrup: Juice 1 cup of fresh blood oranges and 1/2 cup of sugar

In 2020 I made the conscious decision to no longer put off my goals. I noticed that my old associates were being replaced with new likeminded people. Everyone around me motivated me to be comfortable with change because they'd walked in the same shoes or been there before. I don't take the preparation for my journey and the paths that I never knew I'd be ready for, for granted. Don't ignore the signs that some doors have to close in order to walk into the doors where your destiny resides. Everything happens for a reason so don't question God, instead pray for understanding.

I've always been inspired by creativity. When you have the ability to create something amazing, it indicates your passion. Finding new ways to be different helps you stand out so be consistent. One day I picked up a stout beer and just stared at it. For several hours I couldn't figure out how to create a good cocktail out of it. I was definitely outside my comfort zone but with the help of trial and error, I recreated the Moscow Mule using ingredients that I didn't know would work. I wanted the rich chocolate flavors to stand out, but also added a slight spice taste to in order to create a nice balance of flavors. The Beer Master is the perfect example of standing out.

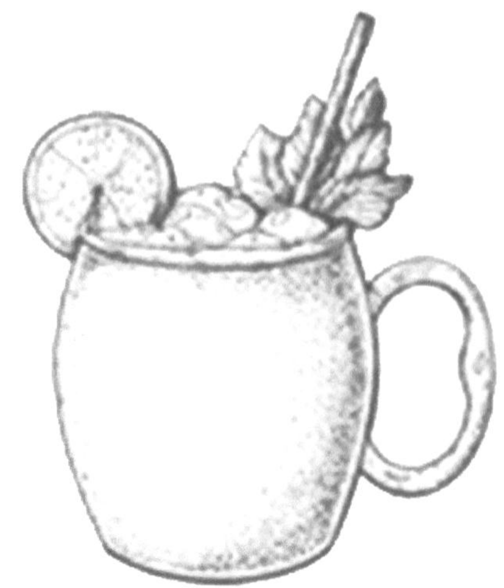

The Beer Master

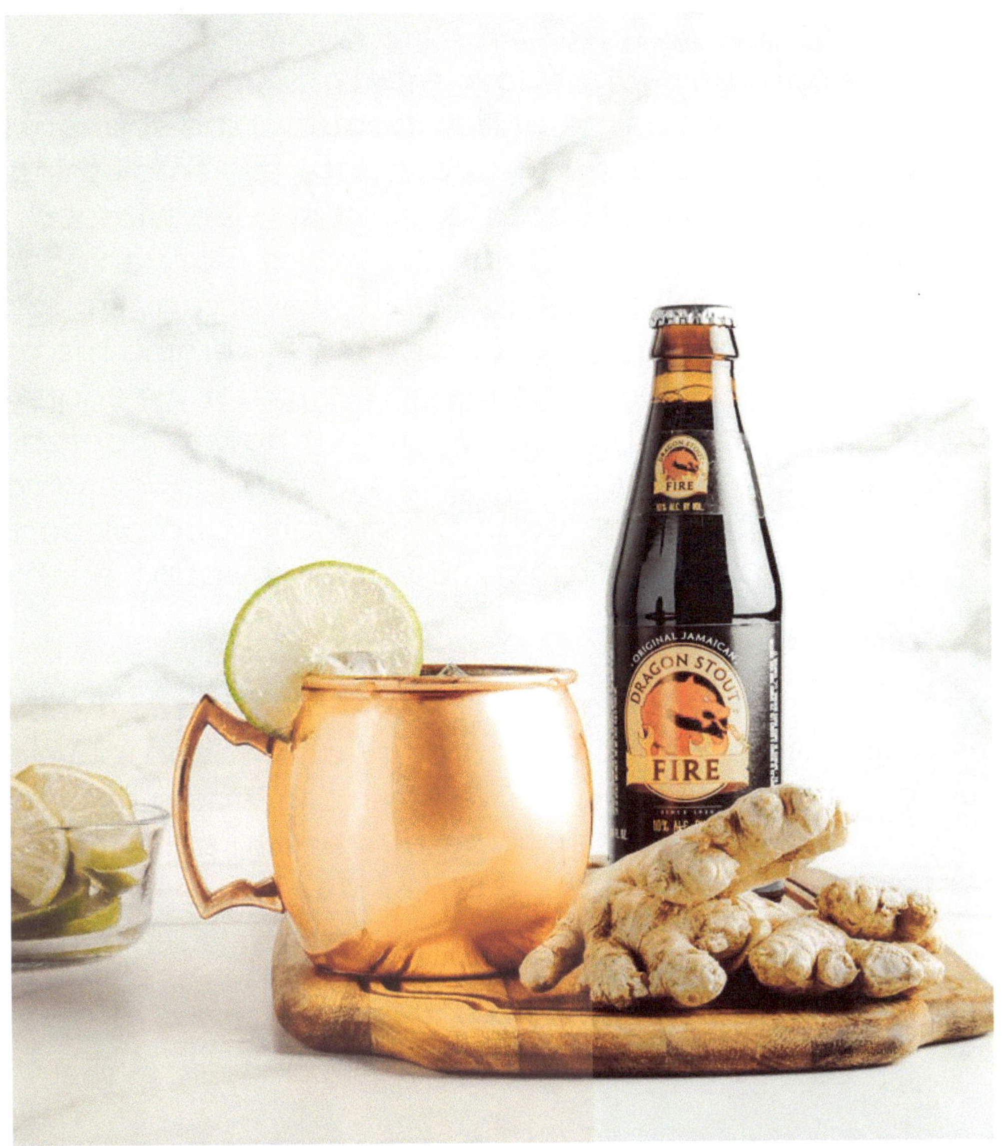

Ingredients:	Instructions:
• 1.5oz peanut butter whiskey • 2oz stout beer • Fresh ginger • Ginger beer	• Muddle fresh ginger (to taste) in mixing glass • Add whiskey and stout beer to shaker • Fill with ice and stir until ice dilutes • Add fresh ice to mule mug • Strain and top with ginger beer • Garnish with lime wheel

The calmness of autumn is what I love most about the season. As I sit in a tranquil space fall reminds me of how beautiful the scenery is around us. Life can be easy if we learn to appreciate the small things around us like nature. Humans forget that we can't survive without nature no matter how we look at it. When I think about the many things that help us survive physically, I can't help but relate my everyday life to the many things happening around me. Friends and family remind me of nature, I couldn't survive without the memories and laughter we share amongst other things. Sometimes as humans we forget how to appreciate each other. We fail to understand one another's love language which makes it very hard to truly appreciate each other. Fall is guaranteed to come every year, we are not! I encourage you to start treating each other like every day is fall.

The 5 ingredients in this cocktail are a representation of the 5 love languages which are quality time, words of affirmation, physical touch, acts of service and receiving gifts. This will serve as a reminder to you that it's truly important to treat each other like nature treats us. We need each other to get through this thing called life.

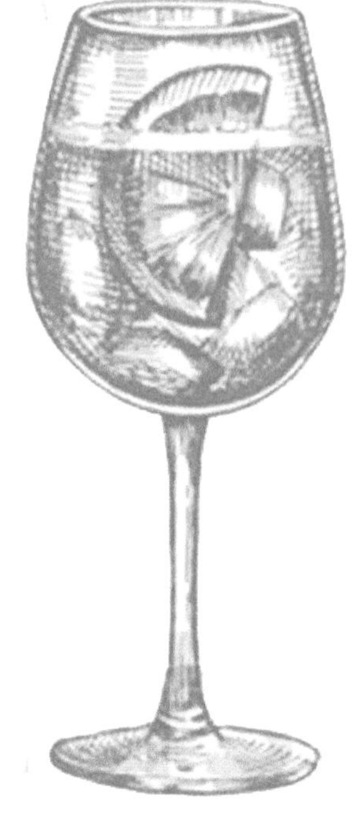

Mother Nature

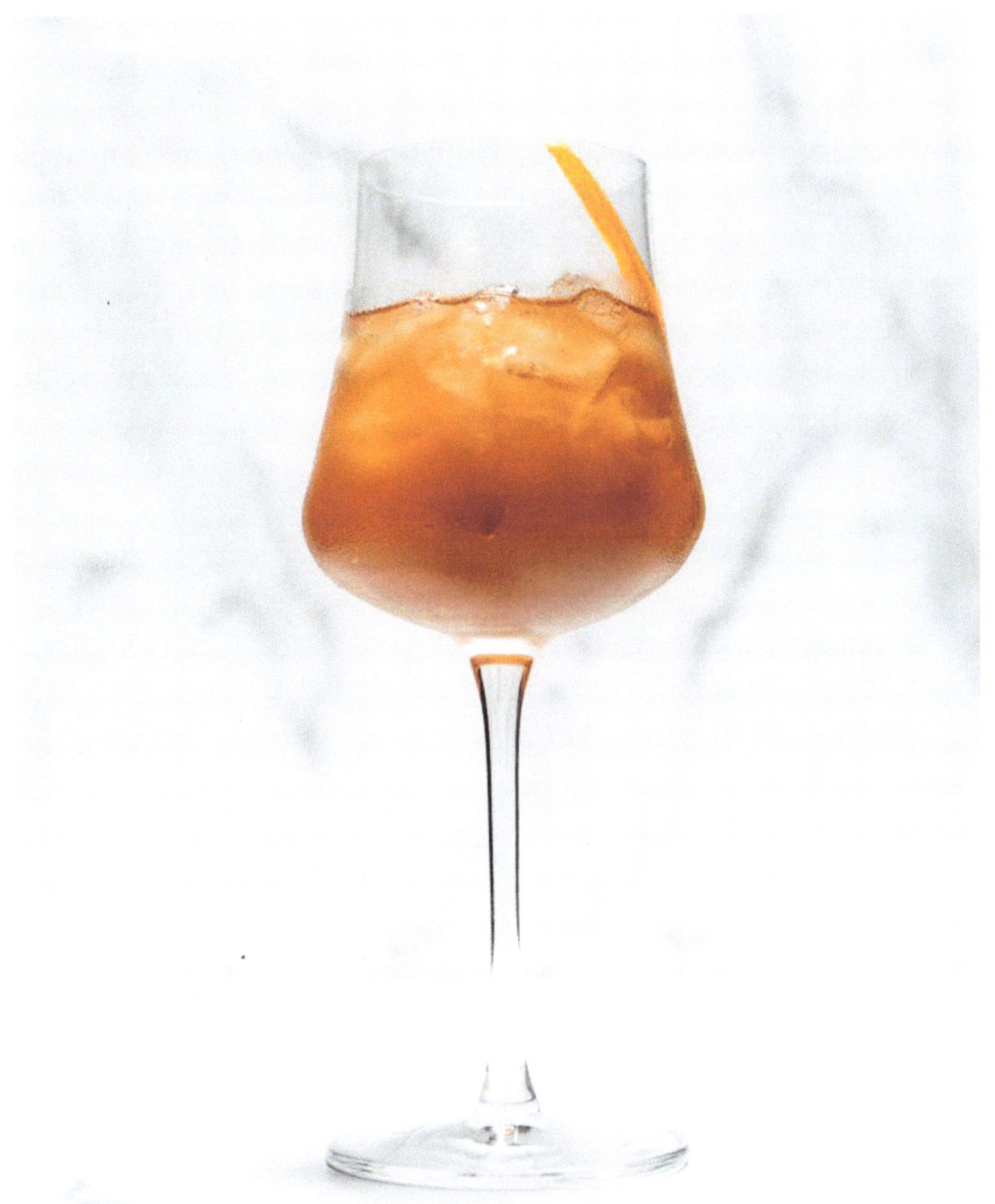

Ingredients:	Instructions:
• 2oz Gin • ¾oz hoodoo • .5oz peach de vagne • .25oz honey syrup • .5oz lime	• Add all ingredients to shaker • Add ice and shake until ice dilutes • Straight from the shaker pour cocktail into wine glass using the dirty ice • Garnish with orange peel

It could be difficult to change who you are as a person, especially when the world is telling you to change. I'll be the first to say that I hate doing things when I'm told to do them. Nobody wants to actually look deep into their hearts and souls to delve real issues until you can no longer run from them. I appreciate the ones who can keep it real with me and tell me that it's time to make changes within myself. Look at how beautiful the trees look during fall. With the proper preparation, we can be just as beautiful.

We all need a push when we're going through change. It can be stressful to say the least so I created the perfect fall shooter. You get rum, dessert and a stress reliever all in one shot. I chose to use these specific ingredients because it's perfect for the weather change and the upcoming holidays. Its presentation is good for gatherings and much more.

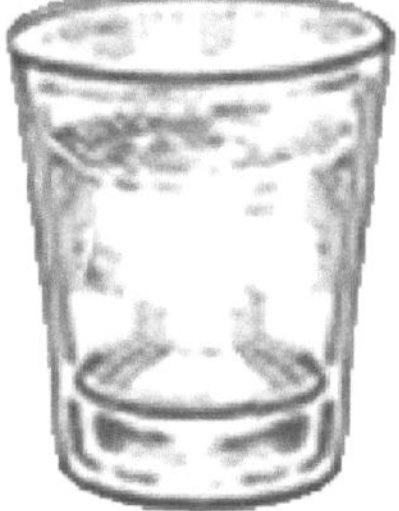
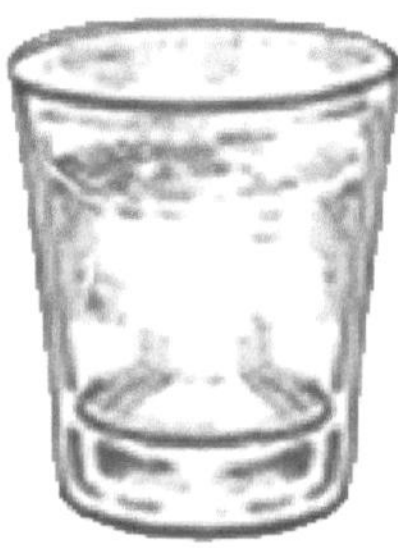

Shot O'clock

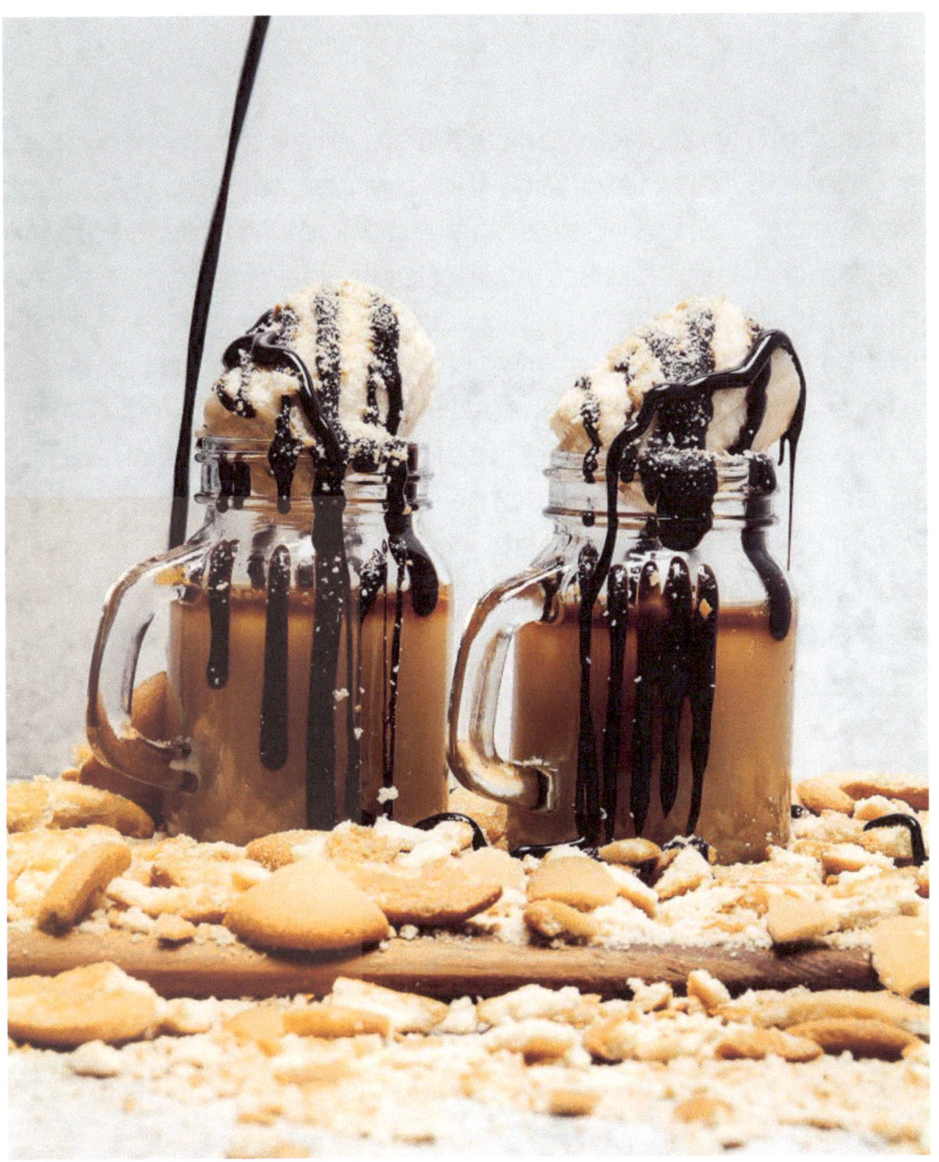

Ingredients:	Instructions:
• 1oz Bacardi gold • 1oz crème de banane • .5oz lemon cheesecake liqueur • ½ banana • 1 spring rosemary • Black rum float	• Muddle banana and rosemary • Add all ingredients except for black rum • Add ice and shake vigorously • Double strain into shot glass • Pour black rum on top slowly to float • Garnish with banana slice and drizzled chocolate

I look at others' stories and wonder how they continue on with life. One of my best friends for instance, I know for a fact that I couldn't walk a mile in her shoes. She was alone and lost in this crazy world having endured losing a mother at a young age, being homeless and a single mother. She was nearly defined by a dark story that made it impossible for the world to see her light shine. No matter how far she came her past always haunted her making her feel like she'd always be stuck there, until one day she had enough. She decided to become an entrepreneur. I'd never seen her so sure about something until I watched her vision and dream happen almost overnight. This was a drastic change in her life, but one that she needed. Her past no longer defines who she is today but is now the push to become a better woman, mother and business owner.

You can't go wrong with a sangria that changes your mood when you drink it. Just like my friend's story this cocktail goes from not knowing where it's going to being the best sangria you've ever had. You have your scotch giving you smokey, chartreuse giving you bitter, juice and fruit giving you sweet and a nice wine to bring it all together. I hope you trust your future enough to overcome your past. We all have to be knocked down to see how strong we really are in the end.

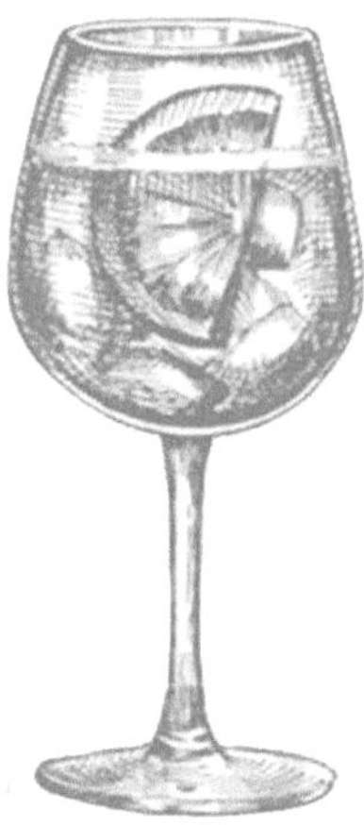

The Light Switch

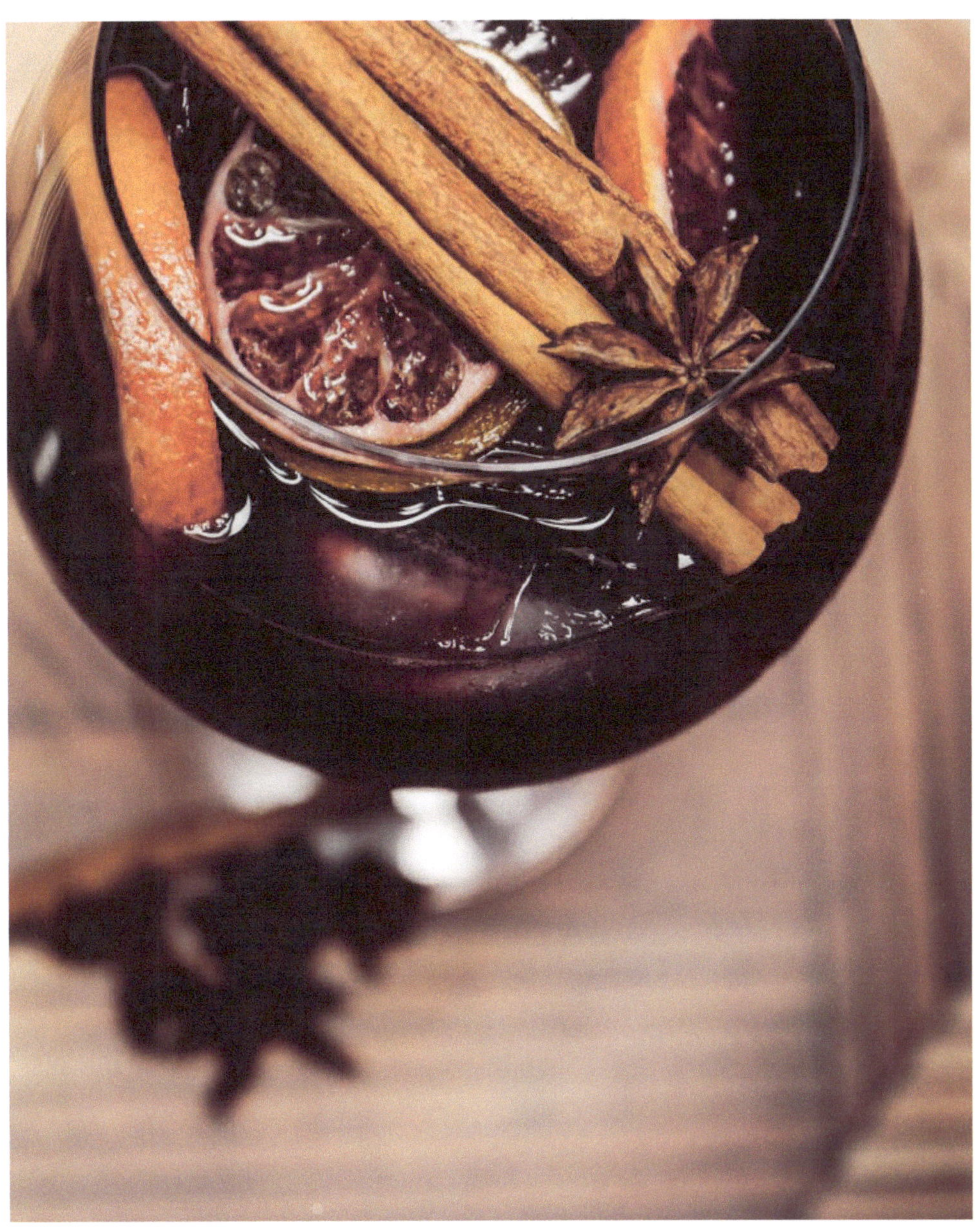

Ingredients:	Instructions:
• 2oz scotch • ¾ oz green chartreuse • 1oz pomegranate juice • .5oz honey syrup • 2 dash chocolate bitters • Tempranillo Wine	• Add all ingredients except wine to shaker • Add ice and shake hard until ice dilutes • Fill wine glass with fresh ice • Strain cocktail over ice • Top with wine • Garnish with fresh fruit, cinnamon sticks and star anise

Chapter 4
Spring Cleaning

When I think of spring cleaning, I think of cleaning my home from top to bottom. This means touching areas that haven't been maintained in a while, like baseboards, blinds, organizing cabinets and closets, etc. A clean home can nourish your health and the decluttering reduces stress and anxiety. I also like to take this opportunity to do some spring cleaning within myself. Spring is a beautiful season. It has a refreshing feel to it and it gives you relaxing vibes. There's nothing like waking up and feeling refreshed, checking in with your mental health, getting rid of any clutter that may have built up and getting your home as well as yourself in order.

In terms of spring cocktails, you'll find that they're lightweight in flavor. You may have heard of the gin tonic. This is a perfect example of a refreshing cocktail that can be enjoyed all spring long. It's simple but light enough to get you through your spring cleaning without feeling sluggish. Mimosas give me the same feel, so I created one that I think you might enjoy during the decluttering process.

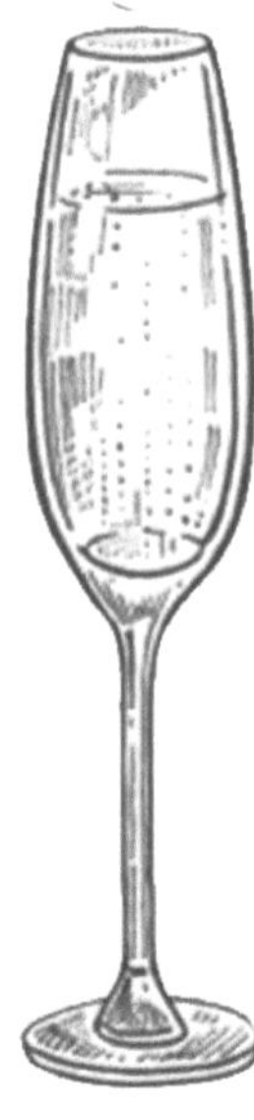

Mimosa Magic

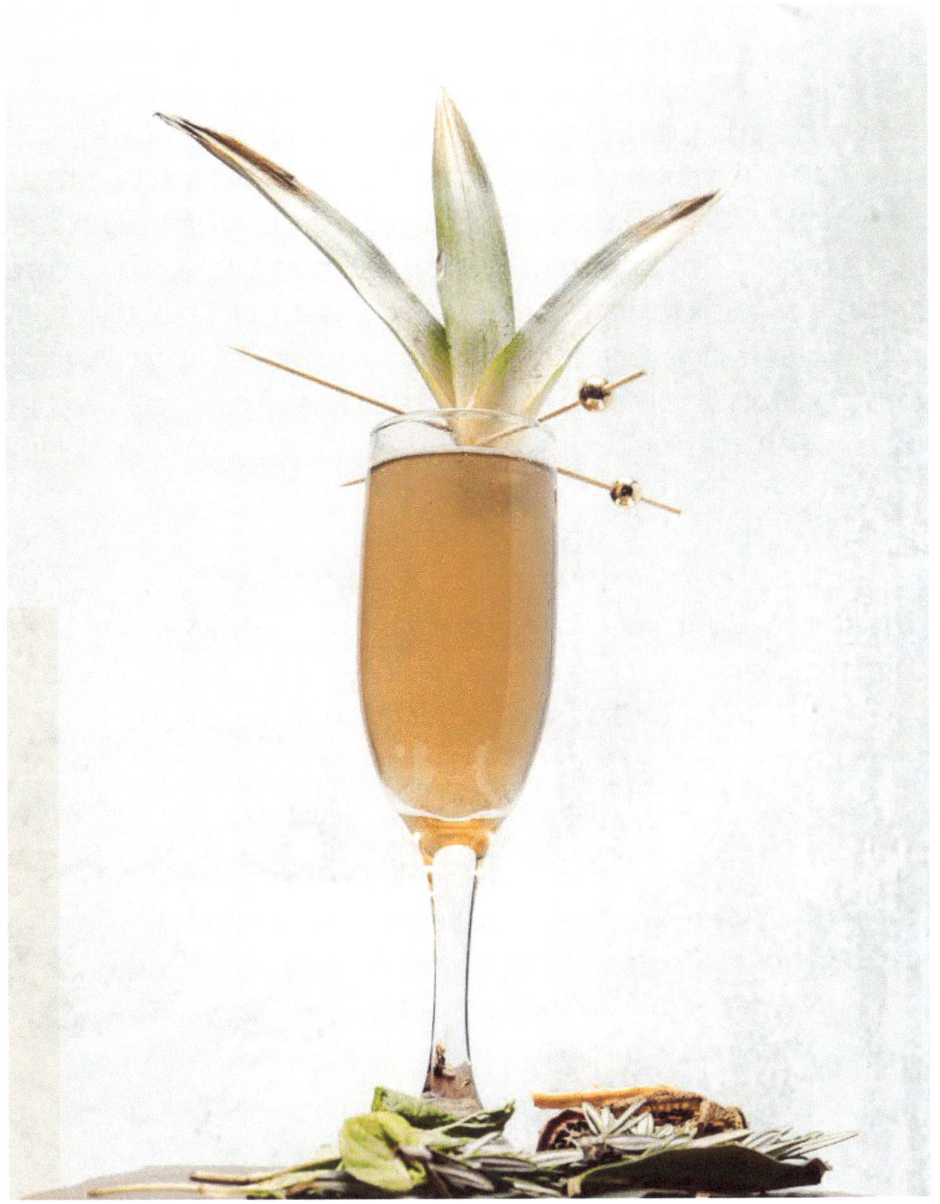

Ingredients:	Instructions:
• 1.5oz cognac • .25oz crème de violete • 1oz fresh green apple juice • .5oz herbacious simple syrup • Top with prosecco	• Add all ingredients to shaker • Add ice and shake until ice dilutes • Strain into flute • Top with prosecco • Garnish with pineapple leaves

Herbacious simple syrup: 1 cup water, 2 cups fresh herbs, 1 cup sugar

One thing I love about working on myself is that I'm working on the best version of me. What's to come is far more important than the things that happened in my past. Yes, it's important to deal with past issues but it's far more important to overcome them. Do the work so it doesn't affect your future. It's so liberating to know that we can be the inspiration for the ones lacking strength. I don't know about you but I want to live out every dream, goal and talent that's within me. The best way to do this is to replace fear with faith.

The Jazzy moon is the very first cocktail that I created with confidence and the first cocktail that many loved. This cocktail was created 3 years ago not knowing that it would give me the confidence to become an author and entrepreneur. This sweet and spicy cocktail is a representation of the woman I am today and also the woman that I'm becoming. Somedays I'm sweet, other days I can be spicy. Most importantly doing the spring cleaning is what helped me along my mixology journey.

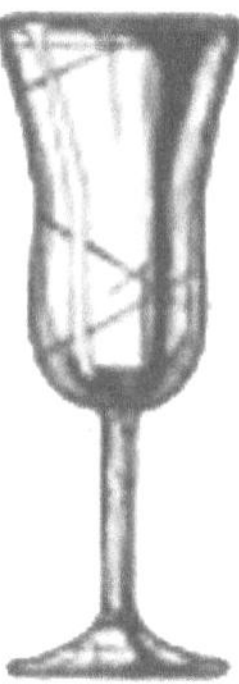

The Jazzy Moon

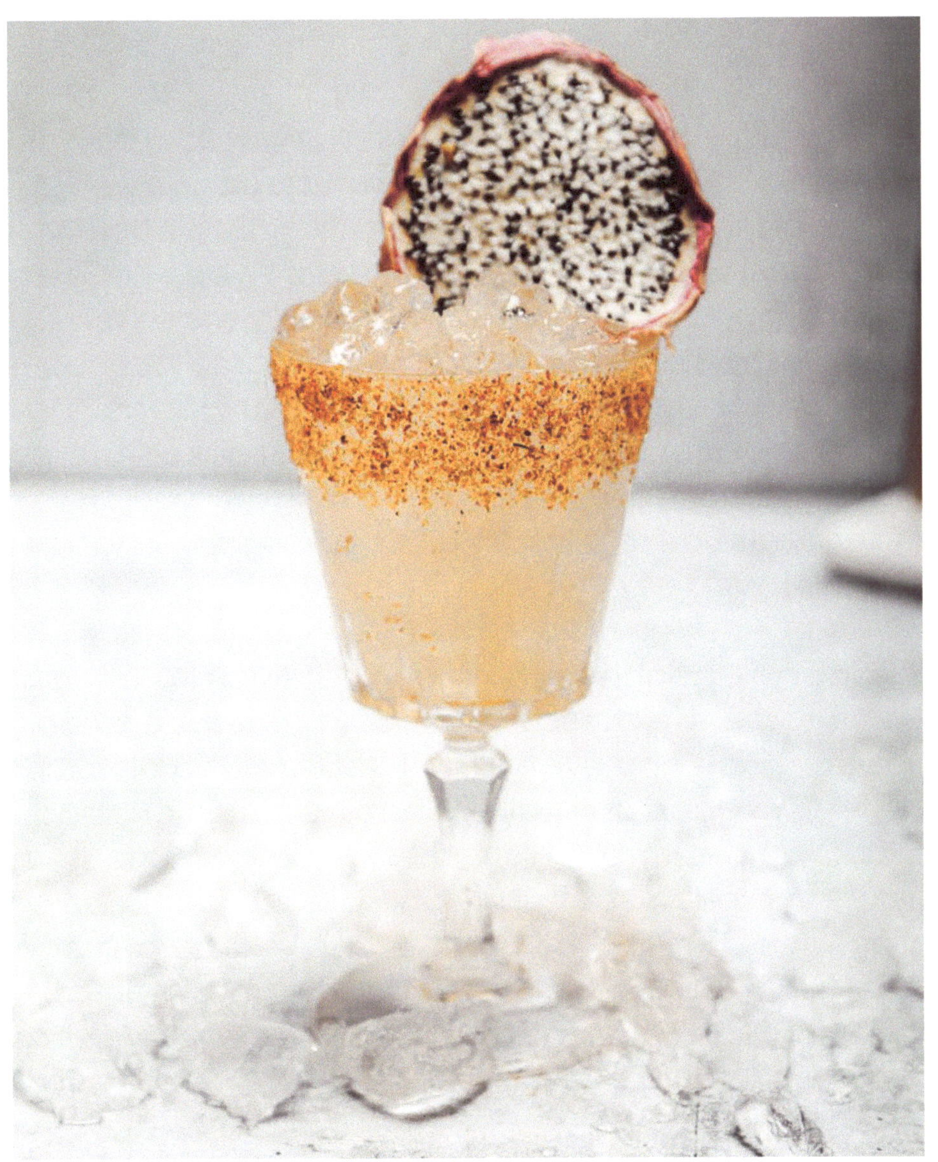

Ingredients:	Instructions:
• 2oz Belle Isle Honey Habanero Mooshine • ¾oz Chambord • .5oz simple syrup • .5oz Lemon juice • Tajin	• Rim glass with Tajin • Add all ingredients to shaker • Add ice and shake until ice dilutes • Add crushed ice to rocks glass • Strain over fresh ice • Garnish with dehydrated dragon fruit

Most of us don't care what people think of us but to a certain extent we should care. I used to be the person who thought everyone else was wrong and I was always the right one. The truth is people viewed me as the complete opposite of who I thought I was. I wasn't everyone's favorite person at one point and it wasn't a coincidence. When it came to my attitude it was anything but accommodating. How could I aspire to be a woman of love and motivation if my energy was saying otherwise? Sometimes, it's not about us, it's about how we make others feel around us. Being fearless doesn't mean having it all figured out. It means taking what others see that you're blind to and making the changes to become a better you.

Detoxing, meditation, healthy eating and fasting are all things you can partake in to become the person we should all aspire to be. The goal is to become better each and every day. Feeling good physically is just as important as feeling good mentally. What we put in our bodies determines how we get through life day by day. The best way to focus on oneself is cutting out distractions and alcohol could be one of them. So, here's a great cocktail that can be enjoyed as a mocktail. Simply take out the alcohol. Both teas in this cocktail have great health benefits to get you through the spring season. Remember others' opinions may not always be false. These moments of focusing on ourselves are vital in order to grow.

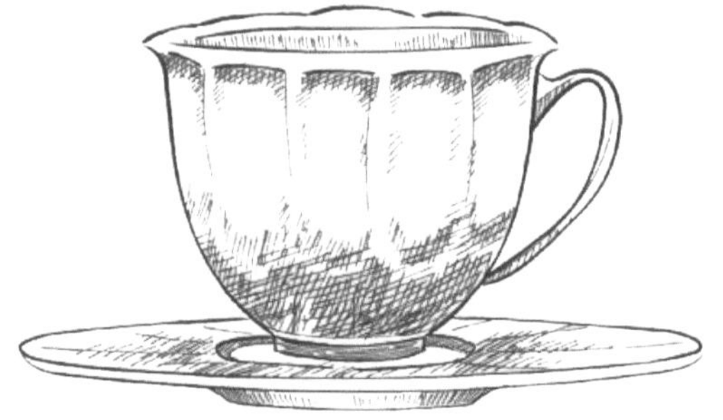

Tea Time

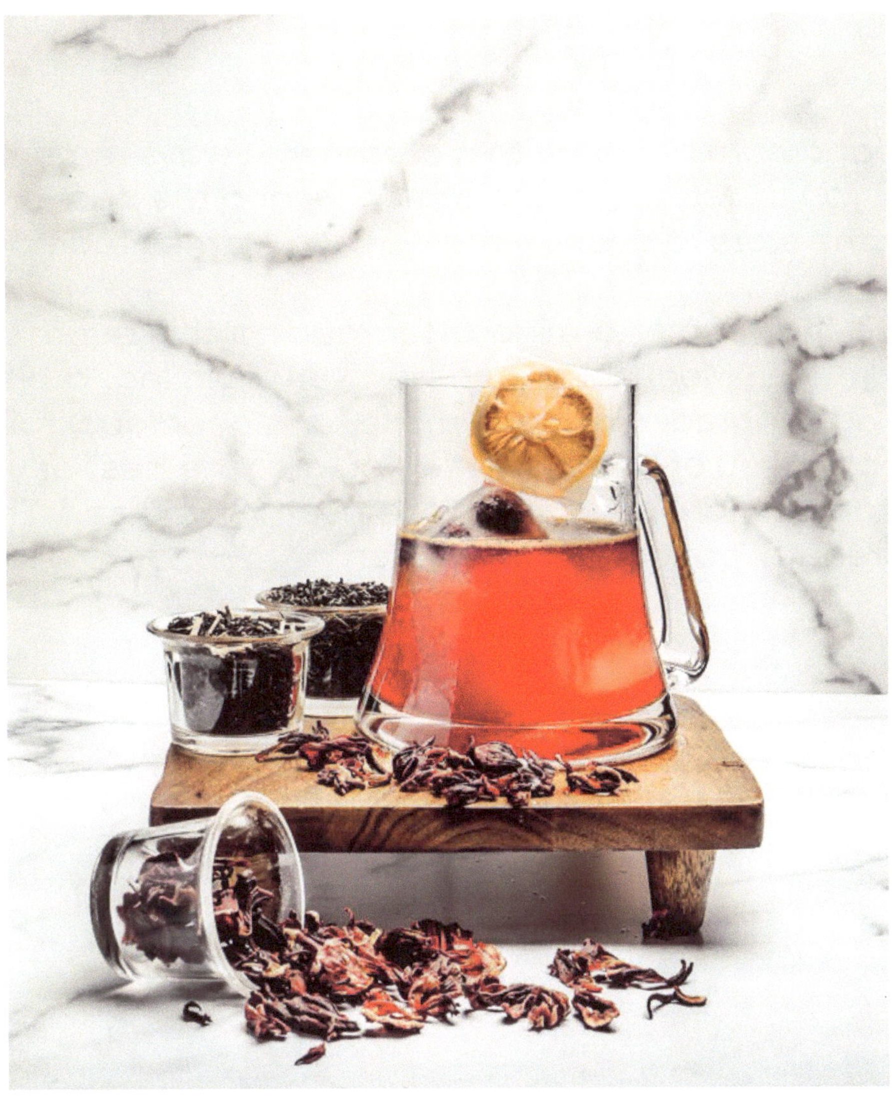

Ingredients:	Instructions:
• 1.5oz gin • 2oz Riesling white wine • 2oz jasmine green tea • 1oz hibiscus tea • 1oz fresh green apple juice • 3/4oz agave	• Freeze fruit into large ice cubes over night • Add all ingredients to shaker • Add ice and shake hard • Stack large ice cubes into glass • Strain over ice

Green tea: ½ cup fresh Jasmine green tea, 1 cup water, ½ cup sugar
Hibiscus tea: 1 cup of Hibiscus flowers, 1 cup water, ½ cup sugar

"Every great dream begins with a dreamer. Always remember, you have within you the strength, the patience, and the passion to reach for the stars to change the world" - Harriet Tubman

The first spirit that came to mind after reading this quote was Moonshine. Just like you, Moonshine can be overwhelming, a bit too much but with the right ingredients it can make for a good cocktail. Allow this season to remind you of how powerful you are. The best of you is yet to come. All it takes is for you wanting the best for yourself. This cocktail embodies strength, patience and passion.

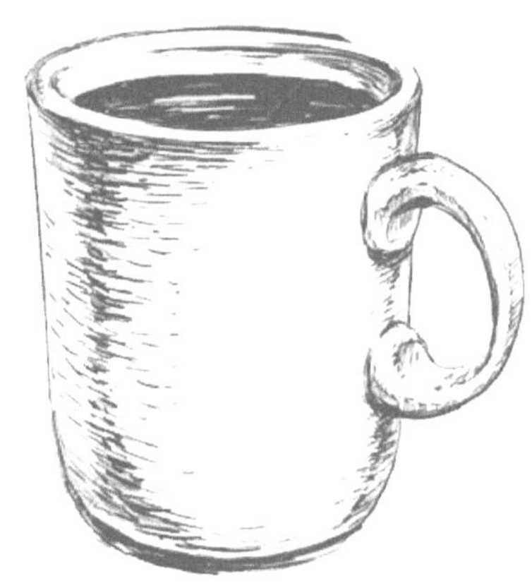

Star-Gazer

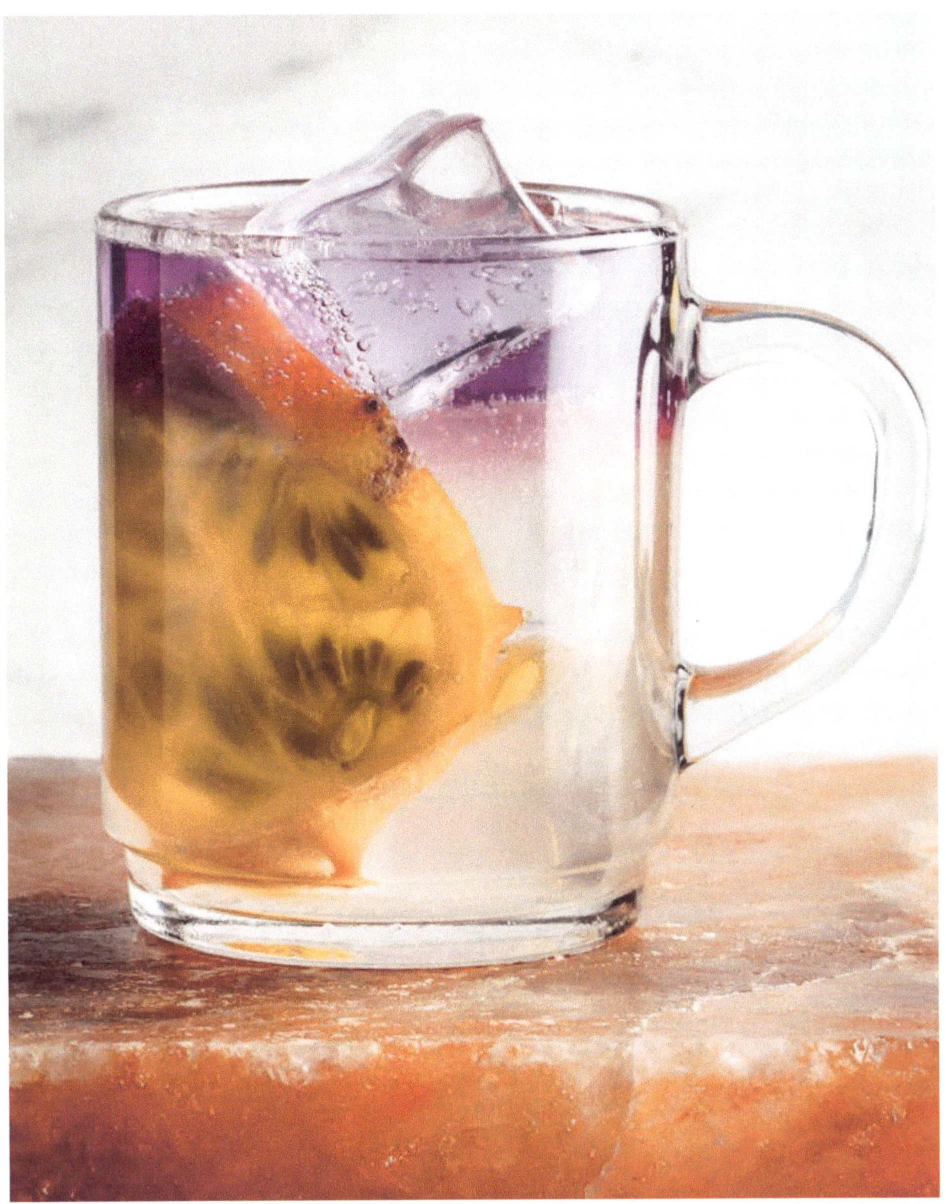

Ingredients:	Instructions:
• 1.5oz Real moonshine • 2oz Elderflower and Rose Cordial • 3/4oz lemon juice • .5oz simple syrup • Butterfly pea	• Add all ingredients to shaker • Add ice and shake vigorously • Add fresh ice to rocks glass • Strain over ice • Add butterfly pea float to finish • Garnish with your favorite fruit

With all that being said, the spring-cleaning process should be embedded in you. Nobody should be okay with staying the same when there are so many opportunities out here. I encourage you to leave any job that no longer sees your worth, leave any relationship that has no future in it and most importantly make sure your mental health is in check. Life is a gamble. Every decision we make has a consequence. We can choose to be happy or not. The choice is yours!

What I love most about craft cocktails is that you can have a different experience everywhere you go. Whether it's at a restaurant or on vacation you'll never try the same thing twice unless of course it's a classic. The inspiration behind this cocktail is my love for avocado. I've had my fair share of visiting restaurants and bars just for the cocktails and never had one with avocado in it so I made my own recipe and absolutely loved it. It's smooth and its flavors are very light tasting making it very easy for my nondrinkers to love it without the negative after effects of alcohol. Trying new cocktails has been therapeutic for me. It reminds me to chase after change rather than running from it. I know that this cocktail will give you that extra push that you've been craving. Whether you like it or not at least you can say you tried it.

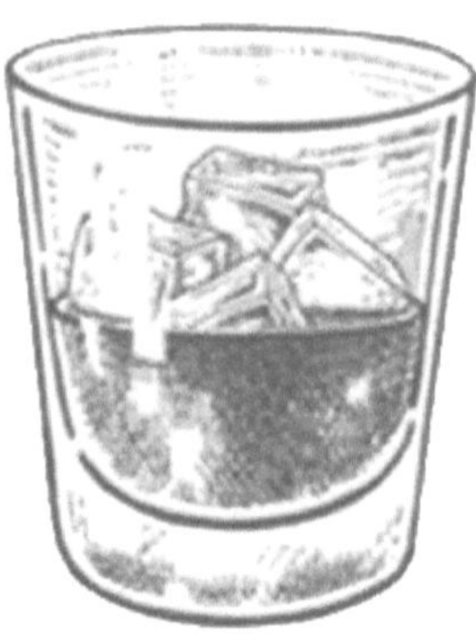

Do or Die

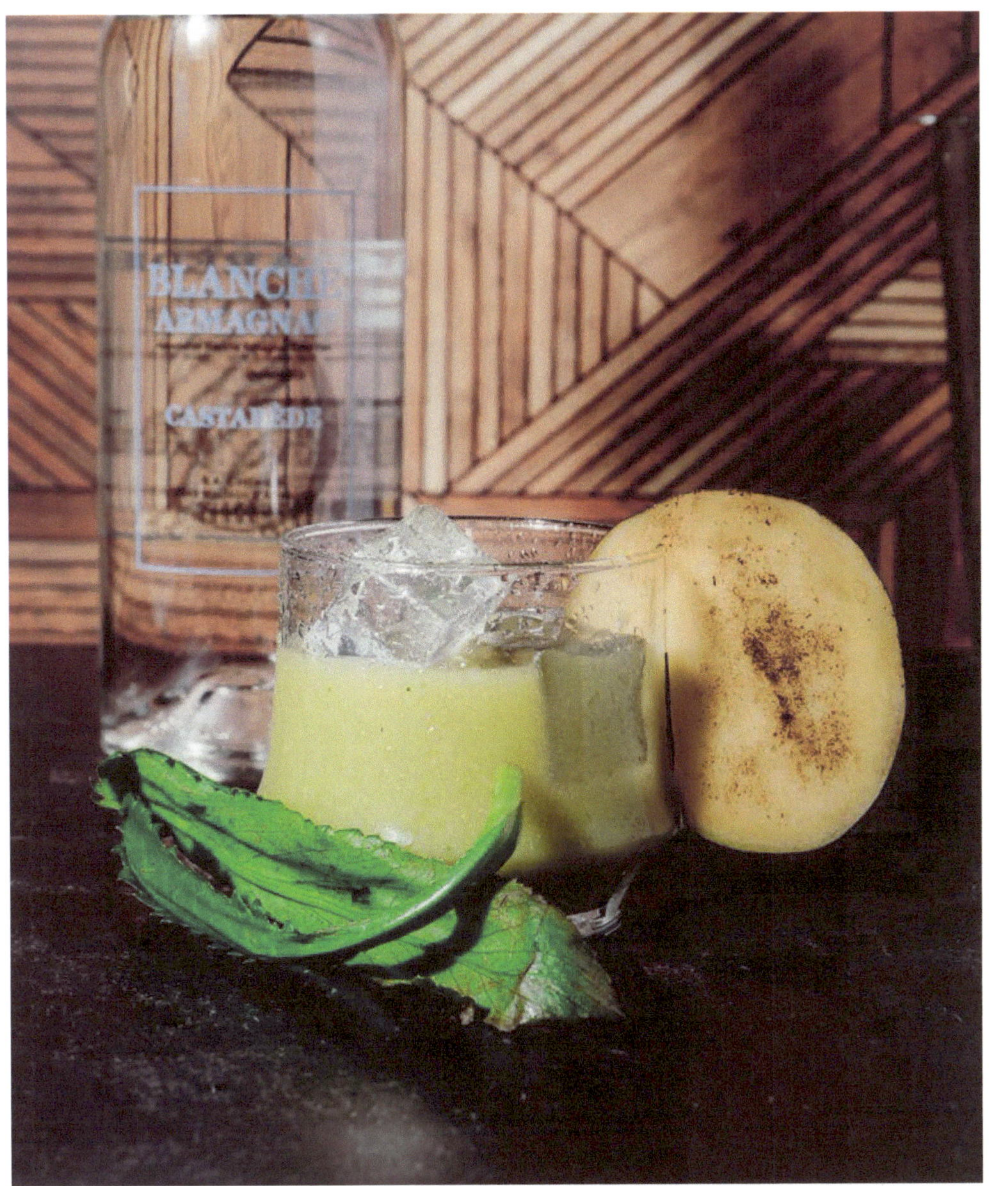

Ingredients:

- 1.5oz Brandy
- ¾oz dry curaçao
- 2oz fresh pineapple juice
- 1oz fresh lime juice
- 2tsp raw honey
- ½ avocado
- 1 whole mango
- 4 leaves culantro (2 leaves if fresh)

Instructions:

- Add all ingredients to blender
- Add a small amount of ice
- Blend until smooth
- Fill rocks glass with ice
- Double strain into rocks glass (use bar spoon to help strain if too thick)
- Garnish with charred mango

Chapter 5
Baby it's Cold Outside

Winter gives us a push forward from previous seasons lack. It's the season that gives us a fresh start. We all set goals we want to accomplish in the new year with hopes that we really make it happen. I'm the queen of starting things and never finishing them so I get excited every new year. It's traditional for everyone to set goals for themselves. The hardest part is sticking to it. If it's freezing outside and we don't put a jacket on, we will be cold. This is how we have to think about our goals. If we don't put our ideas to the test, we are cheating ourselves of success.

Hot drinks are my favorite! They're calming and keep you warm. In the spirit of getting ready for a new year, I figured I'd create a nice boozy hot chocolate. It's a nice treat for those of us who have already put our goals into play.

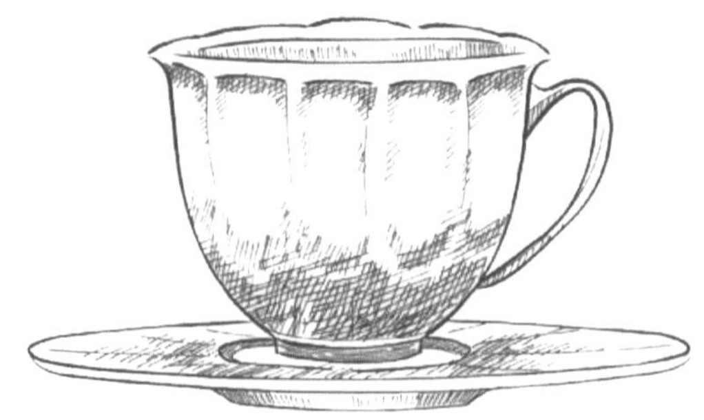

Delightful BonBon

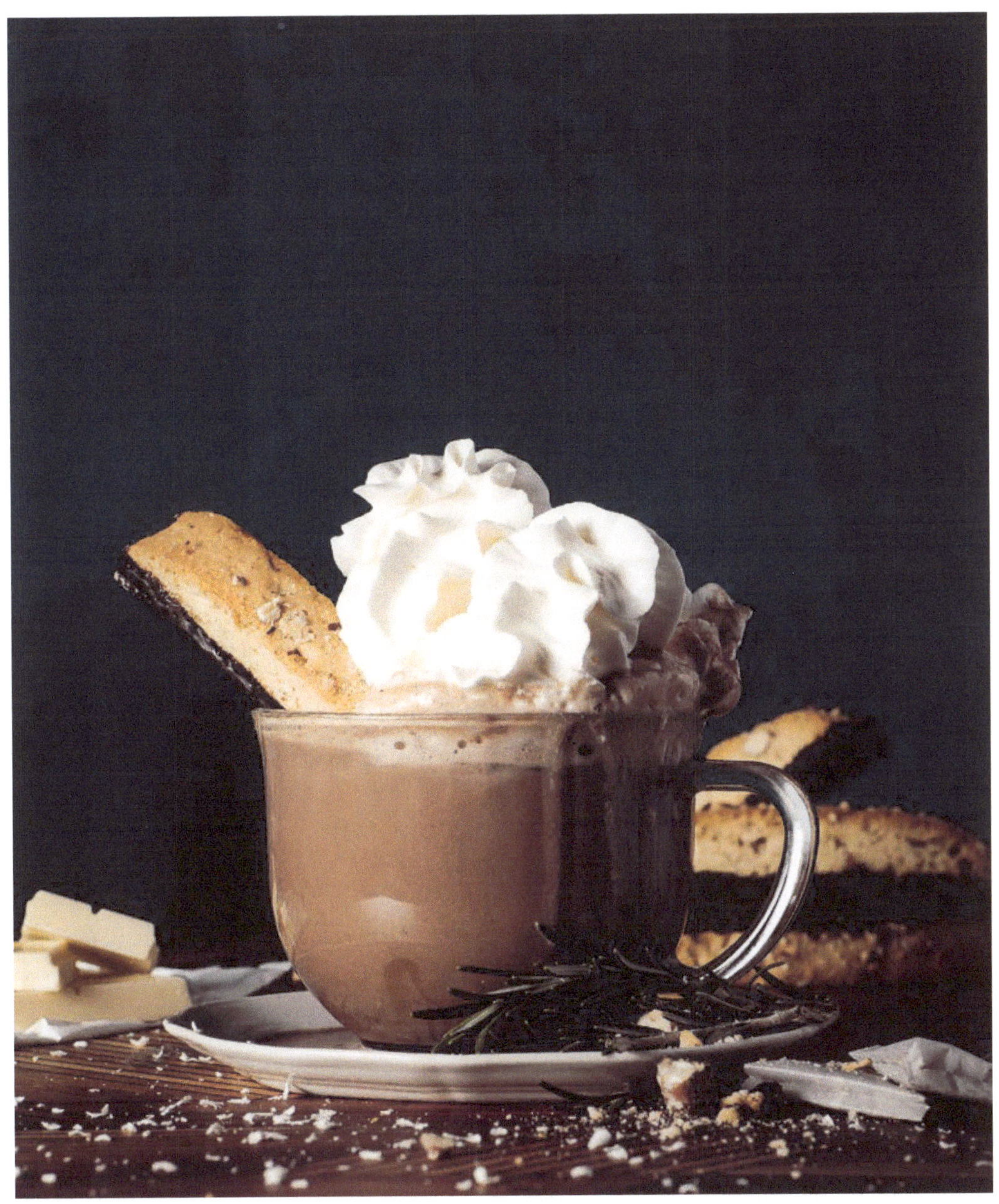

Ingredients:	Instructions:
• 2oz cognac • 1oz Gentiane- Quina aperitif • Dash of vanilla extract • Chamomile Honey Vanilla Tea • Hot chocolate packet • 8oz milk • Fresh Rosemary	• Add milk to small pot and let simmer • Add hot chocolate packet and stir • Add tea bag and 1 drop of vanilla extract • Add 1 spring of fresh rosemary • Let all ingredients simmer • Pour directly from pot into mug • Garnish with whip cream and cookie

New year's resolutions mean nothing if you don't have a plan. One of my best friends is a nail Tech. When she decided to become an entrepreneur, I noticed she started to buy product. She bought tools to get her started at home. She didn't know where the little things would take her but she kept buying product. Ten nail polishes turned into twenty, twenty turned into fifty, fifty turned into a desk and a chair and all of the other tools and products needed to have a successful nail salon. It was a lot of work yes, but she didn't stop at ten nail polishes. She saw it all the way through because she had a plan.

The closest people to you can be the inspiration you need to focus on your plan. I am a living witness of watching a dream start from nothing and blossom into something real, including my own dreams. A cocktail with vodka is safe for most but being safe isn't always the answer. Sometimes you have to jump into the deep end to prove to yourself that you're capable of swimming. When you come back up you will see that it was all worth it. So, in the spirit of diving in the deep end, dive into this recreation of the long island. Multiple spirits in one cocktail can be scary so I gave you tequila from blanco to mezcal. I hope this is the cocktails that reminds you to start the plan and stick to it.

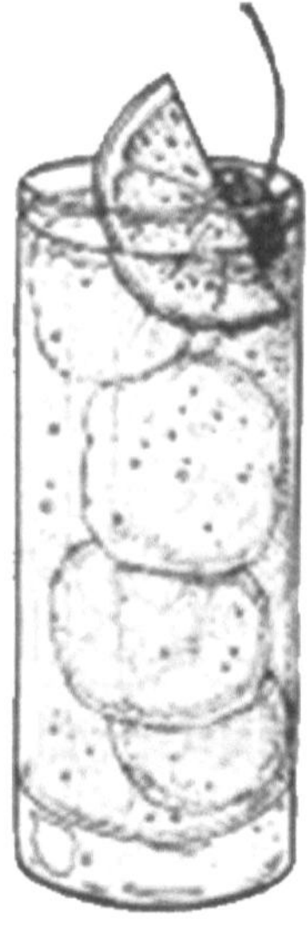

Tequila's Secret Island

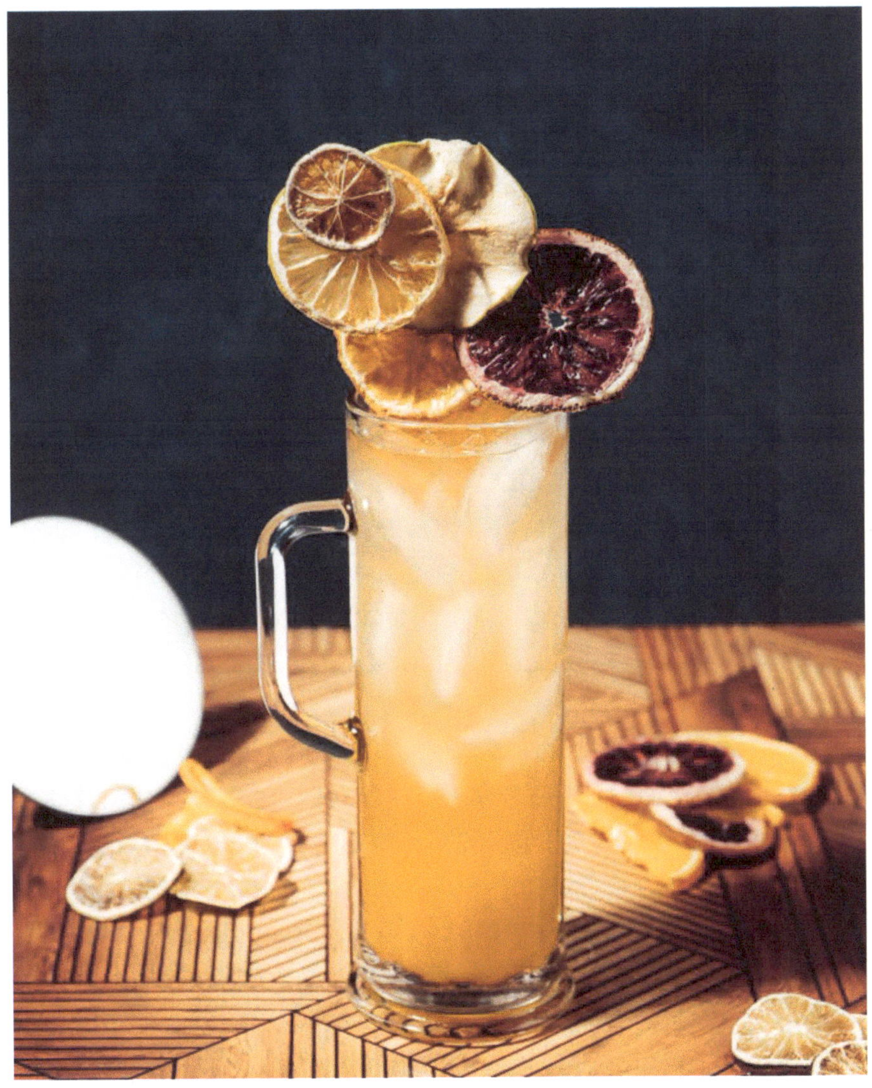

Ingredients:	Instructions:
• ½ oz blanco tequila • ½ oz reposado tequila • ½ oz anejo tequila • ½ oz mezcal • ½ oz grapefruit tequila • 2 oz fresh tangerine juice • 1oz fresh lime • Top with soda water	• Add all ingredients into highball glass • Fill with ice • Top with soda water • Garnish with dehydrated fruits

Make an agreement with yourself that you'll do your best in maintaining your strength and faith. Oftentimes we let the weight of the world determine our happiness when we're the only one that can determine that for ourselves. How you feel about yourself may not be what others think of you but that's why it's important to love yourself the same way that God loves us. We don't always get what we want in life and that's to be expected. We're not ready to face the truth so it's easier to be negative towards anything that doesn't quite make sense to us at the moment. One thing we must understand is that doors open but doors also close and I can bet my last dime that it's always for the best. Prayers are answered immediately sometimes and other times it takes longer than we anticipated. This is where faith comes in. Sometimes making yourself a casual cocktail and letting go will do the trick to moving on with your day. Maybe! Maybe not! Truth is, it's easier said than done. One thing I do know is that taking just a little of your focus off of the things that have you frazzled and putting it in God's hands goes a long way. Enjoy these cocktails like they're your last shot to letting go and living better.

We all have a purpose in life and most of us don't just wake up knowing what that looks like. There are trials along the way that set us back but that's all it is. What's for you is for you...remember that! Cocktails are my therapy. When they're good it allows me to take a deep breath and realize what I have in that moment. We take for granted what God has already blessed us with because we are so focused on what we want or what we think we need. When creating this cocktail, I thought about foods that I've loved my whole life, foods that wouldn't disappoint me if I chose to eat them every day. It was simple, the Pear. It's been my favorite fruit since I was a child and although I don't eat it every day it's something that I'm eternally grateful for. This is the cocktail that helps me take a step back and appreciate all the small things and the accomplishments that have already happened. Let's all be cheerful all season long!

Royal Pearadise

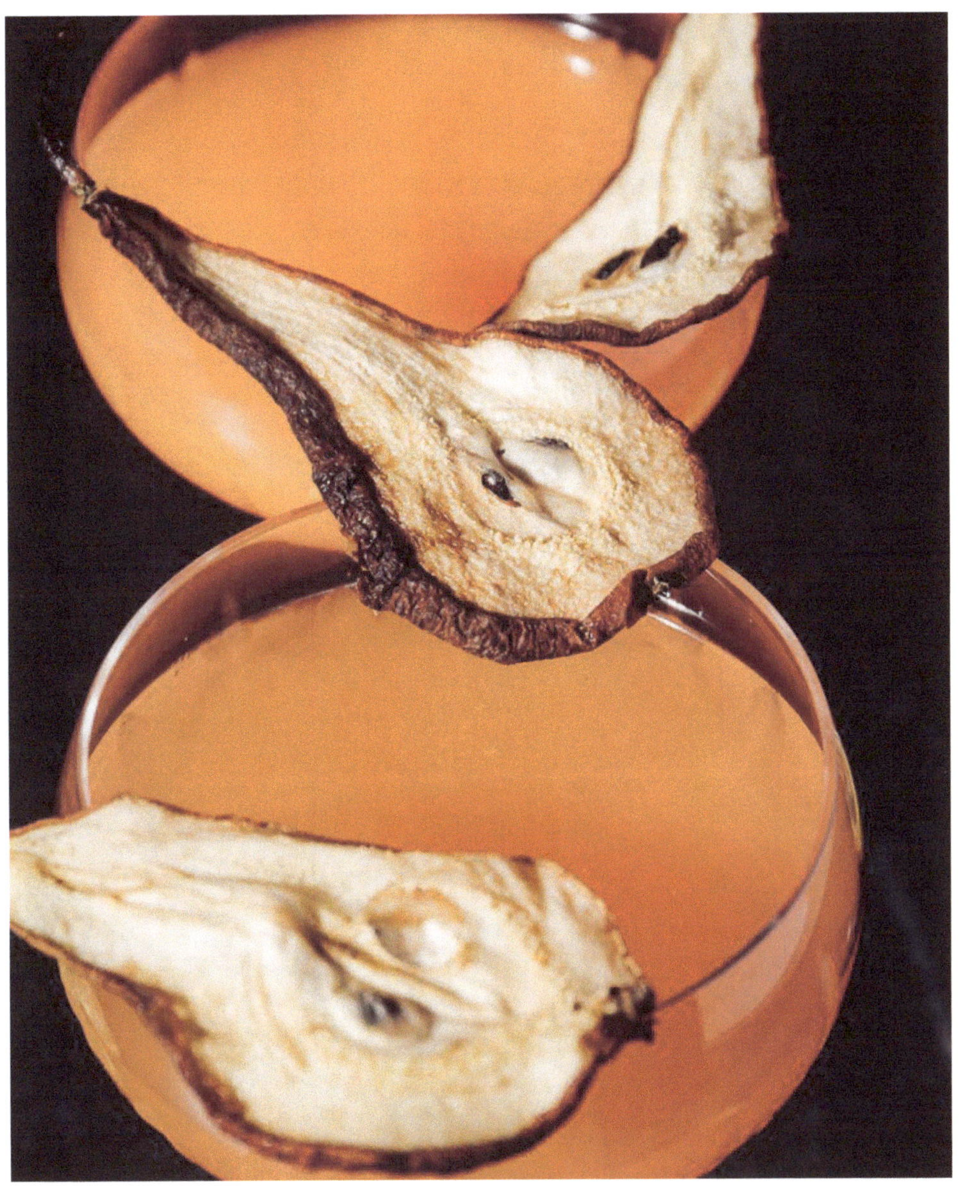

Ingredients:	Instructions:
• 1.5oz Gin • .5 oz green chartreuse • .5oz yellow chartreuse • 1oz spiced pear liqueur • 1oz fresh orange carrot juice • .5oz simple syrup • .5oz fresh lemon juice	• Add ice to coupe glass to chill • Add all ingredients to shaker • Fill shaker with ice • Shake until ice dilutes • Dump ice out of coupe glass • Double strain into coupe glass • Garnish with dehydrated pear

I hate being cold, but I can't stay in the house all winter long. I'd miss out on the beauty of what winter has to offer. Winter is a celebration of love and being kind to one another. The gifts we receive come from the ones that truly love and care for us. Cooking together for the holidays and the warmness of gatherings can't be bought by money. The beautiful lights and the Christmas trees are a reminder of peace. We are forced to show our love towards one another. We are forced to embody the holiday spirit because the gift of love is all around us.

With all of the quality time we spend together during this season, I figured I'd help you all start a new tradition by incorporating a new dessert that the whole family can look forward to every year. I bet you've never experienced a dessert quite like this one before. Here is an ice cream cone filled with a cocktail topped with gelato for garnish.

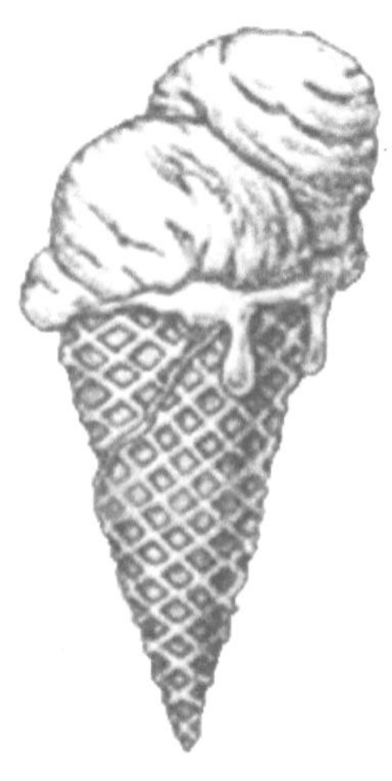

The Gift That Keeps On Giving

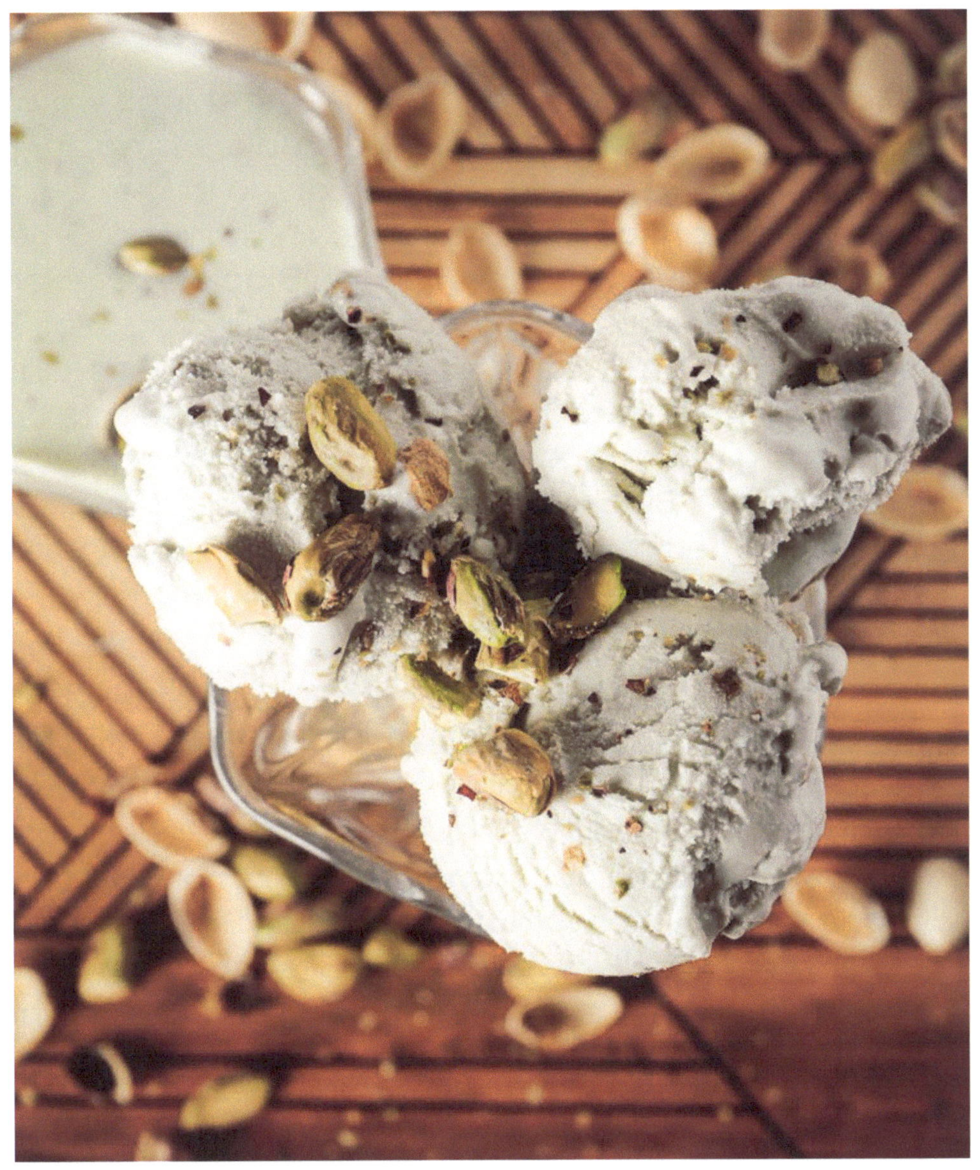

Ingredients:	Instructions:
• 2oz bourbon • 3/4oz midori • .25oz blue cacao • ½ cup fresh pineapple chunks • 1 large scoop of pistachio nut gelato	• Add all ingredients into blender • Add small amount of ice to chill • Blend for about 15 seconds • Pour into ice cream cone • Garnish with a scoop of gelato and pistachio nuts • Add straw and enjoy

Losing a loved one is probably one of the hardest things we all have to endure. The pain doesn't go away, time just makes it easier. Holidays brings family together so when a loved one can no longer participate it hurts. I wanted to shed light on the Black Lives Matter movement because the entire world is hurting over all the Black lives taken from us in plain sight. No family should have to bear this kind of pain. No family should have to lose a son or a daughter due to a senseless killing. I want my voice to be heard so I created a cocktail that represents our culture for everyone mourning during these hard times. In this cocktail you will find ingredients that are Black owned and Black inspired. Along with this cocktail I wrote a poem to the ones that are no longer with us.

"I can't breathe" is why we are all here. The person who was supposed to protect you was causing the trauma. It's so much drama due to your pain. It's so much drama due to this lame white man who didn't see that you were a king. When God created you, he created me. How can I not stand in your name. God took your rib and made me into the woman I am today. So you damn right I'm angry. Another black life taken for no reason. Season after season, year after year when will the bad dreams of another king taken from us disappear. It sucks because it's not a dream this is our reality. I wish I could have picked you up off that ground myself and told you to breathe, breathe, breathe. You deserved to be a father, a brother and a friend but your life was taken. When will this all end?

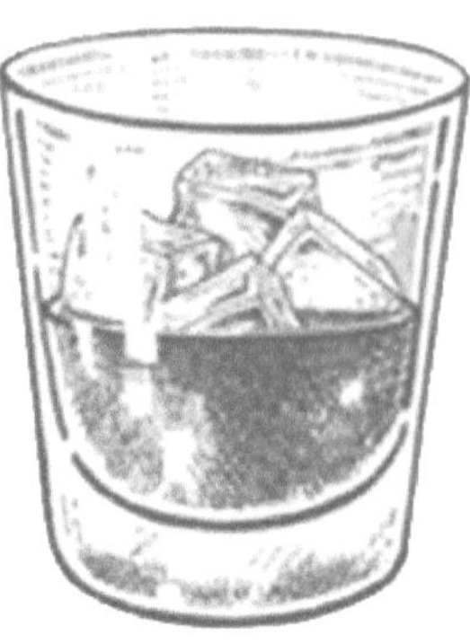

#BlackLivesMatter

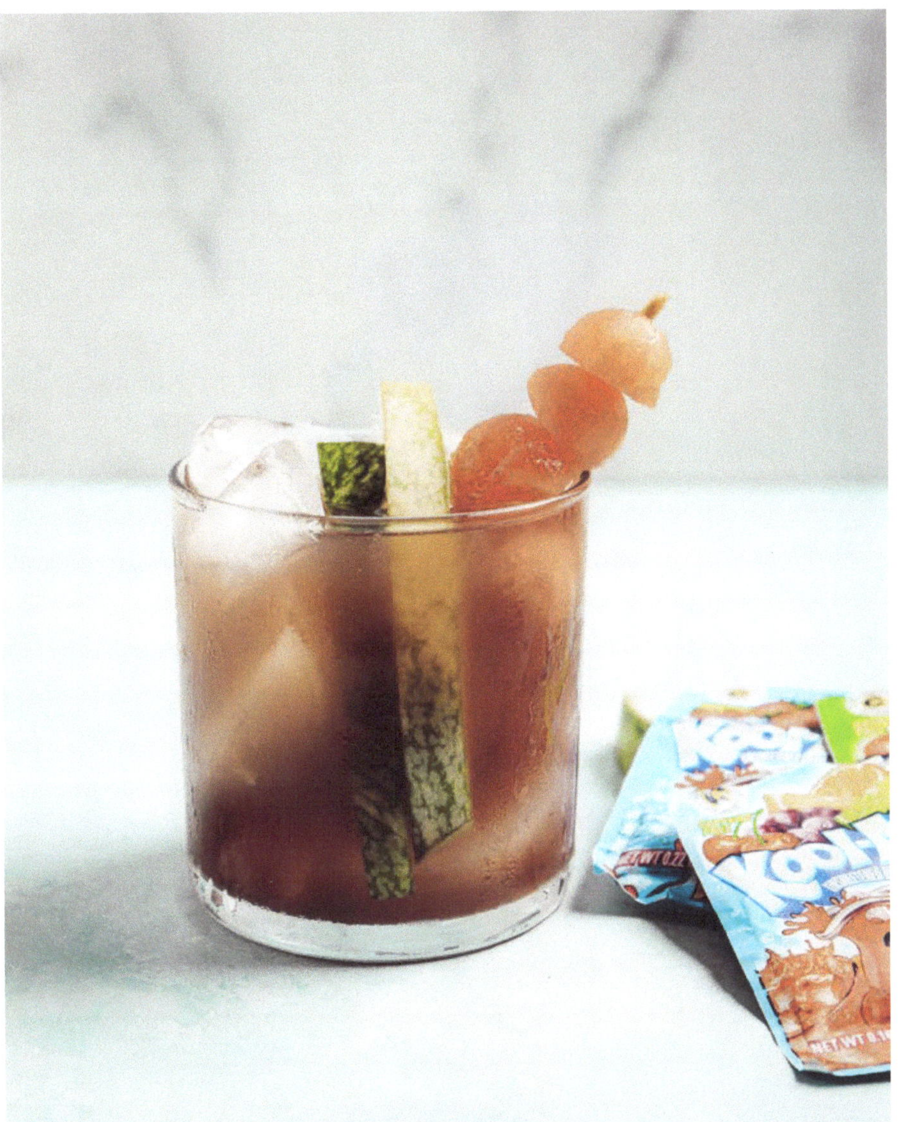

Ingredients:	Instructions:
• 1oz Uncle Nearest Whiskey • 1oz Honey Jack Daniels • 3oz kool-aid • 1oz simple syrup • 3/4oz fresh lime juice • Black girl magic Brut • Fresh watermelon	• Add 1 cup of watermelon to saker and muddle • Add all other ingredients except for brut to the shaker and shake vigorously • Fill with fresh ice into rocks glass • Double strain over ice • Top with Brut • Garnish with watermelon balls
Kool-aid mixer: strawberry kiwi, tropical punch, berry punch	

THE

END

Acknowledgements

First and foremost, I would like to thank God. Without you, I would not have found the courage to write this book. You replaced my fear with faith and guided me through this entire process. Every tear and every prayer went unnoticed and I'm beyond grateful. When I wanted to give up, you reminded me of my wisdom. You have shown me that when I put my trust in you, all things are possible. Thank you for granting me favor on this journey. God, I give you all the honor and praise. For all the glory belongs to you.

I would like to acknowledge my mother Audrey for her never-ending love and support. Truly, you have been an amazing mother since the beginning. Your work ethic and strength has taught me how to persevere, even through the hard times. You have been a listening ear and encouraged me to keep going throughout this entire process. Thank you for my upbringing and teaching me how to build my foundation in Christ. Thank you for showing me the beauty in the storm. You are a strong woman and the reason why I strive to be better each and every day. I love you and I am beyond blessed to have a mother such as you.

To my amazing best friends, Shanae Weeks and Michelle Jones. We've been friends for over a decade and I can truly say that you ladies have become my sisters. From the day I decided to write this book you have been nothing less than supportive. You have tasted an immense number of cocktails, listened to my ideas and pumped me up to keep going when I doubted myself. Thank you for your ideas that you've shared with me to make this book better. Thank you for teaching me the true meaning of sisterhood. Thank you for reminding me of my beauty within and to be myself even when people saw different. Thank you for being my cheerleaders during every trial and test that was thrown my way. We are the definition of black girl magic! I love you girls more than you know.

Last but not least, I would like to thank my work husband and mentor Cody Griffis. Without a doubt, if it wasn't for you taking me under your wing, I would not be the mixologist and author I am today. Thank you for helping me find my passion. Thank you for dragging me to every event to gain knowledge to perfect my craft. Thank you for being patient and believing in me. I'm sorry for all the days I gave you a hard time but I appreciate the bond that came from it. You are truly a gem! I thank God every day that he placed you in my life when he did. I couldn't have asked for a better mentor and friend. I love you lots.

Izzy.cocktails@gmail.com

www.ingramcontent.com/pod-product-compliance
Lightning Source LLC
LaVergne TN
LVHW071630100826
845154LV00007BA/127
* 9 7 8 0 5 7 8 9 3 6 8 0 2 *